SO YOU THINK YOU KNOW LEMONY SNICKET

Clive Gifford

Hodder
Children's
Books

A division of Hodder Headline Limited

© Hodder Children's Books 2004

Published in Great Britain in 2004
by Hodder Children's Books

Editor: Vic Parker
Design by Fiona Webb
Cover design: Hodder Children's Books

The right of Clive Gifford to be identified as the author of the work has
been asserted by him in accordance with the Copyright, Designs and
Patents Act 1988.

10 9 8 7 6 5 4 3 2 1

ISBN: 0340881887

Printed by Bookmarque Ltd, Croydon, Surrey

The paper and board used in this paperback by Hodder Children's Books
are natural recyclable products made from wood grown in sustainable
forests. The manufacturing processes conform to the environmental
regulations of the country of origin.

Hodder Children's Books
a division of Hodder Headline Limited
338 Euston Road
London NW1 3BH

CONTENTS

INTRODUCTION

So you think you know all there is to know about the writings of Lemony Snicket and his tales of the desperately unlucky lives of the three Baudelaire orphans? Reckon you can recall all of Count Olaf's cunning disguises and evil plans, all of Violet's wonderful inventions, and all of the unfortunate scrapes and predicaments – that's a word meaning terrible traps set by Count Olaf – that the children get into? This book contains 1,050 questions, divided into quizzes of 50 questions each. The symbol beside each question isn't a secret code from the V.F.D. or from Isadora and Duncan. It's just to show which book each question comes from. You'll need to be as sharp as Count Olaf's long knife, as tough as Sunny's oversized teeth and as well-read as Klaus to tackle these terrible, tragic, tortuous quizzes.

About the author

Clive is not an orphan, although he was adopted. He has known hard times, such as when he broke both of his arms (his left in eight places) two days before a birthday when he was to receive a junior drum kit. He was never much of an inventor – the patent for his goldfish-powered motorbike was never granted – but, just like Klaus, he's an avid reader, peering at books through his thick specs. Clive is the author of dozens of books for children including *Pants Attack, The Water Puppets* and other titles in the *So You Think You Know . . .* series on *Harry Potter, The Lord of the Rings, The Simpsons, TV Soaps* and *Premier League Football.* He lives in Manchester with his wife, Jane, and their cat Reg.

Key of Titles

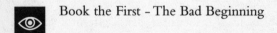 Book the First – The Bad Beginning

Book the Second – The Reptile Room

Book the Third – The Wide Window

Book the Fourth – The Miserable Mill

Book the Fifth – The Austere Academy

Book the Sixth – The Ersatz Elevator

Book the Seventh – The Vile Village

Book the Eighth – The Hostile Hospital

Book the Ninth – The Carnivorous Carnival

Book the Tenth – The Slippery Slope

The Unauthorized Biography and general questions

EXCRUCIATINGLY EASY QUESTIONS

1   What is the surname of the children who became orphans in *The Bad Beginning*?

2   The title of the eighth book in *A Series of Unfortunate Events* is *The Vile Village*, *The Miserable Mill* or *The Hostile Hospital*?

3   Which character in the Lemony Snicket books has just one long eyebrow?

4   Which one of the Baudelaire children is a budding inventor: Sunny, Violet or Klaus?

5   In *The Reptile Room*, who does Stephano turn out to be?

6   Who used their strong teeth to climb up the walls of the elevator shaft?

7   How many Baudelaire children are there: two, three or five?

8   What sort of creature does Dr Montgomery study in his laboratory?

9 In *The Vile Village*, what type of bird covered the buildings in V.F.D.?

 10 When Verdant Flammable Devices are lit, what colour smoke do they give out?

 11 What were the workers at the Lucky Smells Lumbermill fed for lunch: oatmeal, peaches or chewing gum?

 12 In *The Wide Window*, what was the name of the aunt with whom the Baudelaire children were to stay?

 13 What is the name of the hunchbacked man at the carnival: Roger, Hugo or Kevin?

 14 Which of the Baudelaire children wears glasses?

 15 Which musical instrument does Vice Principal Nero play?

 16 What is the name of the village handyman: Hal, Duncan, Hector or Edgar?

 17 Dr Montgomery is the children's dead father's cousins' wife's brother. What does he tell the children to call him?

EXCRUCIATINGLY EASY QUESTIONS

18 Is the Lucky Smells Lumbermill found in the town of Lake Lachrymose, Paltryville or Briny Beach?

19 In *The Ersatz Elevator*, who organises the In Auction every year?

20 What is the name of the old man who works in the Library of Records: Ed, Hal, Paul or Griff?

21 What is the name of the teacher in *The Austere Academy* who is really Count Olaf in disguise?

22 Who is the eldest Baudelaire child in the Lemony Snicket books?

23 There are pictures of a certain type of fish on the walls and menus of Café Salmonella. Which fish is this?

24 In *The Wide Window*, who packed a welcome present in each of the children's trunks?

25 Who is the youngest of the Baudelaire children?

26 What job did Lemony Snicket do on a newspaper: was he a designer, a theatre critic or a crime reporter?

27 In *The Carnivorous Carnival*, who does Count Olaf mention has a crystal ball?

28 What is the punishment for breaking rules in V.F.D. village: five years in prison, a fine, burning at the stake or writing 100 lines?

29 How many of the three Baudelaire children are girls?

30 In *The Wide Window*, Count Olaf disguises himself as a sailor. What name does he go by?

31 The children see an eye symbol on a Snow Scout's backpack. Which three letters can be found in the eye symbol if someone looks very, very closely?

32 In *The Miserable Mill*, Dr Orwell is really Count Olaf in disguise: true or false?

33 In *The Wide Window*, which town do the Baudelaire children travel to in its off season?

34 In *The Bad Beginning*, how many teeth does Sunny Baudelaire have?

35 Which teacher in *The Austere Academy* wears a turban on his head?

36 The two white-faced women refused Count Olaf's orders to throw Sunny off the mountain top and they left his troupe: true or false?

37 Who killed Gustav, Dr Montgomery's previous assistant?

38 In *The Wide Window*, who bit through Captain Sham's wooden leg to reveal that it was a fake?

39 What did Violet tie together and fashion into a type of bungee cord, in *The Hostile Hospital*?

40 Dr Montgomery's bushes and hedges are trimmed into the shape of what creature?

41 Which eye does Captain Sham's eye patch cover?

42 In *The Vile Village*, who does Officer Luciana turn out to be?

43 Mr Poe asked Stephano to show him his ankle. What was he looking for?

44 While Sunny, Violet and Klaus are at Prufrock Preparatory School, in what sort of building are they to live?

45 What type of cutlery did Violet tie to the children's shoes to enable them to climb up the frozen waterfall?

46 In *The Reptile Room*, what food item did the Alaskan Cow Lizard produce?

47 Who in *The Vile Village* wore a pair of green boots with lightning flashes?

48 Did Madame Lulu hire or refuse to hire the Baudelaire children disguised as freaks?

49 Whose glasses were broken at the Lucky Smells Lumbermill?

50 Where on his body does Count Olaf have a tattoo?

MISERABLY MEDIUM QUESTIONS

QUIZ 1

1 Across which body of water did the Fickle Ferry travel in *The Wide Window*?

2 What is the highest temperature that Esmé and Jerome Squalor's oven can be heated to: 300 degrees, 400 degrees, 500 degrees or 600 degrees Fahrenheit?

3 On the first night that Klaus, Sunny and Violet spent in the lumbermill, what was for dinner: lasagna, beef casserole, chewing gum or oatmeal?

4 Violet fashioned a lockpick from an electric plug on an item in her room. Was this item: a lamp, an electric clock or a radio?

5 In *The Reptile Room*, who discovered and named the Incredibly Deadly Viper?

6 In Lemony Snicket's unauthorized autobiography, whose wedding motto was: 'Married after only one evening together'?

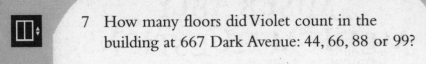

7   How many floors did Violet count in the building at 667 Dark Avenue: 44, 66, 88 or 99?

8   According to Hector, what does 'V.F.D.' stand for in V.F.D. village?

9   Who, in *The Austere Academy*, took Klaus, Violet and Sunny to the boarding school?

10 In *The Wide Window*, who said that English grammar was her greatest joy?

11 Who met the angry mob of V.F.D. villagers while riding a turquoise painted motorcycle?

12 As Count Olaf drove through the Mortmain Mountains, who kept on pinching Sunny to be quiet?

13 What is the name of the road that runs from the city to Tedia: Lousy Lane, Tedious Drive, Smelly Street or Wayward Avenue?

14 What did Uncle Monty believe had fallen from Klaus' room and hit him: a canoe, a brass reading lamp or a big book on snakes?

15 Esmé had lunch with 12 millionaires. How many said they were coming to her In Auction?

MISERABLY MEDIUM QUESTIONS

16 In *The Austere Academy*, a certain school building is out of bounds to children. If they are found in it, they have to eat their food without cutlery. Which building is it?

17 Sunny, Violet and Klaus visited Babs' office where they were spoken to through a speaker: true or false?

18 What did Violet set light to in order to make a rescue signal?

19 In *The Miserable Mill*, what is the name of the forest the children pass through on the way to their new home?

20 Who did Klaus and Sunny recognise and follow to the surgical ward: Count Olaf, Babs, Esmé Squalor or Hal?

21 With which hand did Violet sign the marriage document in *The Bad Beginning*?

22 In *The Carnivorous Carnival*, a journalist called Count Olaf 'Your Countship'. The reporter was from which newspaper?

23 According to Lemony Snicket's unauthorized autobiography, how many wigs are contained in the V.F.D. disguise kit?

MISERABLY MEDIUM QUESTIONS

24 As Klaus and Violet pretend to be a
two-headed freak, what item of food
does Count Olaf give them to eat?

25 What item of Violet's did Isadora use to
disguise herself, apart from her shoes?

26 In *The Miserable Mill*, who was ordered to
push a log with a man tied to it into the
saw machine?

27 What was the name of the newspaper that
carried the story of Duncan and Isadora's
capture by Count Olaf?

28 What is the title of the first book in *A Series
of Unfortunate Events*?

29 Which one of Count Olaf's henchmen slept
inside the sailboat renting business: the man
with hooks for hands, the women with white
faces or the person who could be a man or
a woman?

30 Lemony Snicket mentions that he once
had business cards printed to help him escape
from an enemy castle. What did these say he
was: a knight, a French admiral or the King
of Denmark?

31 In the Library of Records, Sunny, Violet and Klaus first started their search in which letter aisle?

32 What colour was the Door Prize trophy in *The Ersatz Elevator*?

33 Who filled up more pages of their notebook trying to come up with a plan to save the Baudelaire children: Isadora or Duncan?

34 At the start of *The Slippery Slope*, where are Klaus and Violet: in a caravan, in the boot of a car or in a cage?

35 Count Olaf orders a pit to be dug by the rollercoaster. What does he want to keep in it?

36 The room the Baudelaire children shared in Count Olaf's house had one painting. What object did it depict?

37 The two Quagmire children were originally triplets. What was the name of their brother who died in a fire?

38 How many hours did Lemony Snicket wait for Dr Sebald in the cinema: six, nine, 13 or 19?

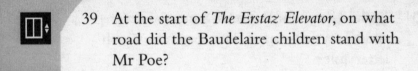

39 At the start of *The Erstaz Elevator*, on what road did the Baudelaire children stand with Mr Poe?

40 When the children were in jail, what item did Hector give them: a metal file, a crowbar, a poem or a screwdriver?

41 What is the title of the second book in *A Series of Unfortunate Events*?

42 Which one of the Baudelaire children had trouble remembering things after a visit to Dr Orwell?

43 What age was Violet when she won her first ever invention competition: five, seven or nine years old?

44 At the start of *The Hostile Hospital*, in front of which general store did the Baudelaire children stop?

45 While Violet, Sunny and Klaus were at Count Olaf's house, who was the first visitor they received?

46 When the Baudelaires left the carnival with Count Olaf and his gang, on whose lap was Sunny sitting?

47 What was the statue in the middle of Fowl Fountain made of: metal, wood, marble or brick?

48 Which letter was on the back of Esmé's red snowsuit?

49 The Baudelaire children hid in the boot of Count Olaf's car. How did air get in?

50 What did Violet put over her face moments before she warned Esmé about the trap?

QUIZ 2

1 What film did Uncle Monty, Stephano, Klaus, Violet and Sunny watch the night before their expedition: *Jaws, Zombies in the Snow* or *The Trials of Olaf*?

2 What subject did the children first search for in the Library of Records: Baudelaire, Jacques, Olaf or Snicket?

3 In *The Carnivorous Carnival*, who cut the line attaching the car to the caravan: Kevin, Mr Poe or Klaus?

4   In *The Bad Beginning*, is the Baudelaire children's new 'father': a Lord, a Baron or a Count?

5   A female contortionist lives in a caravan at the carnival. What is her name?

6   When Violet, Sunny and Klaus are in jail, how many two-line poems do they finally have?

7   According to V.F.D. village's Rule #961, what sort of dessert cannot have more than 15 nuts?

8   What colour was the oven the Baudelaire children used to heat the iron objects: blue, black or red?

9   In *The Miserable Mill*, what is the name of the town which is to be the Baudelaire children's new home?

10   Who ordered Violet, Klaus and Sunny to make dinner for ten members of a theatre troupe?

11   On what object did Klaus, Violet and Quigley haul Esmé to the top of the icy slope?

12   What does S.O.R.E. stand for: Secret Orphan Ruining Exercises, Special Orphan Running Exercises or Sneaky Orphan Recital Exercises?

MISERABLY MEDIUM QUESTIONS

13 Uncle Monty's snake collection includes a pair of snakes who have learned to drive a car: true or false?

14 What is Captain Sham's first name: George, Julio or Frederick?

15 Which one of the following sticky objects did Klaus not find in the caravan cupboards: chewing gum, blackstrap molasses, lemon curd or glue?

16 In *The Ersatz Elevator*, all the money made by the In Auction goes to whom?

17 What is Dr Sebald's first name: Gustav, Frederik or Mikael?

18 The man in charge of moving Uncle Monty's snake and reptile collection woke the children up. Where had they been sleeping?

19 Officer Luciana's third harpoon hit which object: Hector's steering wheel, the balloon basket, the rope ladder or the fuel tank?

20 The building in which the Squalors lived had how many apartments on each floor: one, two or four?

MISERABLY MEDIUM QUESTIONS

21 Which musical instrument did Count Olaf tell the bus driver was contained inside his instrument case?

22 At the start of *The Carnivorous Carnival*, Count Olaf turns his car onto a highway with three words all beginning in 'r'. What is its name?

23 In which part of Count Olaf's house did Sunny, Klaus and Violet spend the last night before they were to appear in the play?

24 In *The Slippery Slope*, what sort of drink did Sunny make Count Olaf and the other villains for breakfast: herbal tea, iced coffee or orange juice?

25 In *The Ersatz Elevator*, the world's second-finest crystal was formed into: a stapler, a vase, a door knob or a globe?

26 Which teacher at Prufrock School had a thick black moustache and constantly ate bananas?

27 In *The Reptile Room*, what is the name of the river which is mainly mud?

28 In *The Austere Academy*, which item of Klaus' did Duncan use to help disguise himself, apart from his shoes?

29　What job in the Lucky Smells Lumbermill occurred after tying: debarking, stamping or sawing?

30　What flavouring did Sunny add to the hot chocolate: peppermint, cinnamon, parsley or orange essence?

31　What is the name of the mountain peak where Count Olaf says his troupe will be camping on their first night away from the carnival?

32　In *The Vile Village*, what did the newspaper say Count Olaf's name was: Oscar, Harry, Omar or Henry?

33　What tea service item is an optional part of the V.F.D. disguise kit?

34　Uncle Monty says that he and the Baudelaire children will work every day until suppertime. Where does he say they will go after supper?

35　At the Last Chance General Store, Klaus, Violet and Sunny escape from the police by climbing into a van driven by a bearded man with a guitar. The man has worked with Volunteers Fighting Disease since the organization was first formed: true or false?

MISERABLY MEDIUM QUESTIONS

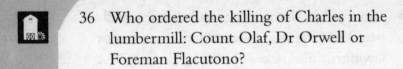

36 Who ordered the killing of Charles in the lumbermill: Count Olaf, Dr Orwell or Foreman Flacutono?

37 Count Olaf imprisons Sunny at the top of a tower. Violet makes a rescuing device, but which of the following does she not use: a curtain rod, picture wire, a bicycle wheel, strips of clothing?

38 What were all the people who lived in the Lucky Smells Lumbermill dormitory covered in?

39 How long is Vice Principal Nero's nightly violin recital: one, two or six hours?

40 For how long has V.F.D. village been known by that name: over 50 years, over 100 years, over 200 years or over 300 years?

41 In *The Wide Window* who managed to get the keys from Count Olaf's assistant whilst they slept in the shack by the docks?

42 Which one of the following items was not advertised on the front of the Last Chance General Store: mango-flavoured sweets, white wine, plastic knives, fresh limes?

43 In *The Carnivorous Carnival*, who offers the freaks a place in Count Olaf's gang if they perform one task?

44 What sort of items would Violet never normally fiddle with: guns, cars, electrical devices or knives?

45 What is the name of the dock where the Baudelaire orphans are sitting on their suitcases at the start of *The Wide Window*?

46 What is the name of the boarding school which Sunny, Violet and Klaus attend in *The Austere Academy*?

47 Which one of the following items is not contained in the V.F.D. disguise kit: fake hands, silver pants, false teeth or a turban?

48 What colour was the car that took the Quagmire children away from Prufrock Preparatory School?

49 *The Wide Window* is the third, fifth or seventh book in *A Series of Unfortunate Events*?

50 What does Klaus say his mother could do with crackers in her mouth: sing, do impressions or whistle?

QUIZ 3

1   In *The Vile Village*, who figures out the coded message from Isadora's poems: Klaus, Violet or Sunny?

2   In *The Miserable Mill*, what was the special word used to command Klaus when he was hypnotized: Snicket, lucky or order?

3   Who was the usual gym teacher at Prufrock School, before she fell out of a window: Miss Carp, Miss Tench, Miss Blowfish or Miss Bream?

4   At the start of *The Reptile Room*, who drove Klaus, Sunny and Violet to Dr Montgomery?

5   What colour ink was used to stamp the wooden boards at the Lucky Smells Lumbermill?

6   In the Library of Records, which was the second letter aisle that the children visited in their search: 's', 'j', 'k' or 'b'?

7   When the Baudelaire children are at Captain Sham's shack, which of them does the mountainous creature lift up first?

8   How many people finally sailed away in Hector's flying machine?

MISERABLY MEDIUM QUESTIONS

9 The Baudelaire children try to find Gunther by listening in on all the apartments, then they have their lunch in the lobby: true or false?

10 *The Bad Beginning* is dedicated to whom?

11 What iron items did Sunny and Klaus collect from the Squalors' living room, with its six fireplaces?

12 In Lemony Snicket's unauthorized autobiography, who was the artist who sent the author a letter containing a sketch of the burnt-down mansion?

13 In *The Slippery Slope*, Violet offers to tell Count Olaf the location of what item in return for Sunny?

14 Aunt Josephine's husband could whistle Beethoven's fourth quartet with crackers in his mouth: true or false?

15 What was the name of the lumbermill foreman that Klaus, Sunny and Violet had to work for?

16 Count Olaf orders the man with hooks for hands to catch what sort of fish for breakfast?

17 The Duchess of Winnipeg's letter to Lemony Snickett was written on: tree bark, a linen napkin, a handkerchief or the inside of a cardboard box?

18 What does Esmé Squalor say to Klaus and Sunny that they may have to do to the hospital?

19 Who does the Last Chance storekeeper say will be delivering a newspaper to him soon: Lou, Stephano, Hal or Paulo?

20 In *The Ersatz Elevator*, where did the children find themselves when they opened the trap door?

21 What game did the freaks in the caravan play to pass the time: snakes and ladders, dominoes, cards or marbles?

22 In a letter at the end of *The Ersatz Elevator*, Lemony Snicket tells his editor he can receive the manuscript for *The Vile Village* if he buys a carton of milk from which store?

23 Coach Ghengis ordered Klaus, Violet and Sunny to paint what shape on the Prufrock School lawn?

24 Which one of the following is not one of the villages in the orphan-raising programme: Tedia, Mountbank, Paltryville, Ophelia?

25 How high is the tower at Count Olaf's home: 10 feet, 20 feet, 30 feet or 40 feet?

26 Which adult in *The Austere Academy* was jealous of the Baudelaire children attending boarding school?

27 On the side of the House of Freaks tent there was a drawing of a girl with how many eyes?

28 How many men in overalls did Klaus, Sunny and Violet see moving the cages of reptiles?

29 Who lied about a phone call from Captain Sham, saying it was from the Hopalong Dancing School?

30 Uncle Monty plans to unveil the Incredibly Deadly Viper as a practical joke to scare: Mr and Mrs Poe, the Herpetological Society or Count Olaf?

31 Which unpleasant girl sat directly behind Violet in her class and often poked her with a stick?

MISERABLY MEDIUM QUESTIONS

32 What is the name of the new fountain in the V.F.D. village?

33 Who was looking through the glass walls of the Reptile Room at Violet trying to unlock Stephano's suitcase?

34 At the hospital, where is the Library of Records located: sixth floor, first floor, third floor or basement?

35 What was the name of the carnival where Madame Lulu was to be found?

36 What item did the children plan to use to take Sunny's place in the running exercises ordered by Coach Ghengis?

37 Which book in *A Series of Unfortunate Events* comes after *The Miserable Mill*?

38 What was the name of the auctioneer who visited the Squalor penthouse one evening?

39 In *The Slippery Slope*, who did Count Olaf order to put up the two tents for his gang?

40 Whose English grammar was the last Aunt Josephine got to correct before she met her end in Lachrymose Lake?

MISERABLY MEDIUM QUESTIONS

41 In which room did the children find Uncle Monty dead?

42 At the start of *The Ersatz Elevator*, who is promoted to Vice President in Charge of Orphan Affairs?

43 At what address does Esmé Squalor live?

44 Are the workers at the lumbermill paid in: chewing gum, shares in the company, coupons or pretend money?

45 Which one of the following ingredients was not in the puttanesca pasta sauce made by the Baudelaire children: garlic, anchovies, green peppers, tomatoes?

46 In Lemony Snicket's unauthorized autobiography, what was the title of the Dr Sebald film featuring zombies?

47 In *The Wide Window*, what sort of sweet did Mr Poe bring the children in a paper bag?

48 How many old women from the Council of Elders came to visit Hector and the children as they were cleaning the Fowl Fountain?

49 At the start of *The Slippery Slope*, who tied hammocks together in the caravan?

50 In *The Hostile Hospital*, Sunny tore a thin strip off her medical coat for Violet to use as what?

QUIZ 4

1 Violet opened the lock of the car boot with a cord attached to what sort of eyewear?

2 Which book in *A Series of Unfortunate Events* comes after *The Ersatz Elevator*?

3 The children stole a bag of flour from what part of the Prufrock School buildings?

4 In *The Slippery Slope*, what did the children use as a drag chute to slow the caravan down?

5 Who instructed Violet and the other children to cook dinner, then got angry when they didn't serve roast beef?

6 What sort of transport took the Baudelaire children within several hours' walk of the village of V.F.D.?

MISERABLY MEDIUM QUESTIONS

7 At the carnival, the children finished their hot chocolate, saw the lions arrive, then headed into which tent?

8 What was the name of the restaurant that Jerome Squalor and the children were to go to at seven o'clock?

9 Babs greeted the children at the front of the Heimlich Hospital with some yellow flowers: true or false?

10 In *The Hostile Hospital*, who do the children send a telegram to from the Last Chance General Store?

11 Which member of staff at the Prufrock Preparatory School always mocked and mimicked the words of the school children?

12 In *The Bad Beginning*, who attempted to arrest Count Olaf after his plan was uncovered at the theatre?

13 'Love Conquers Nearly Everything' was the motto of whose wedding: Lemony and Beatrice, Jacques and Esmé or the Baudelaire children's parents?

MISERABLY MEDIUM QUESTIONS

14 How many visitors arrive at Count Olaf's gang's mountain camp site at breakfast time?

15 Who locked the tall gates to Captain Sham's business, stopping Mr Poe from giving chase?

16 Madame Lulu packed food and important papers to leave the carnival with the Baudelaire children: true or false?

17 What was the name of the teacher at Prufrock School who was obsessed with measuring the size of everyday objects?

18 What kept Foreman Flacutono's shoes together: laces, string, tape or rivets?

19 In *The Ersatz Elevator*, which eating place was hired to provide the food for the In Auction?

20 What landmark in V.F.D. village was used as a prison to hold Isadora and Duncan Quagmire?

21 In Lemony Snicket's unauthorized autobiography, what was the original name of the play, *One Last Warning to Those Who Try to Stand in My Way*?

22 In *The Vile Village*, what did Isadora and
    Duncan drop from the flying machine to help
    Klaus, Violet and Sunny?

23 In *The Miserable Mill*, how many times a day
    does the train stop at Paltryville?

24 Detective Dupin puts the Baudelaire children
    in the dirtiest cell of his jail. What does he
    call it?

25 In *The Ersatz Elevator*, what does the
    doorman say is his real profession: a
    policeman, an actor or a chef?

26 What V.F.D. village landmark were Klaus,
    Violet and Sunny beside when they heard the
    news that Count Olaf had been captured?

27 Mr Poe let Count Olaf escape from Uncle
    Monty's house because Count Olaf paid him:
    true or false?

28 Which eccentric relative in *The Wide Window*
    is afraid of exploding radiators?

29 What material is Dr Montgomery's house
    made of: wood, steel or stone?

30 In *The Ersatz Elevator*, beside which church was Count Olaf's black pick-up truck found?

31 In which room in Aunt Josephine's house was the Wide Window?

32 When the children were searching in the Library of Records, what was the name of the first file that they found and opened?

33 In *The Bad Beginning*, who made a grappling hook out of an old curtain rod?

34 What was Sunny's first chore when they arrived at the mountain campsite: put up the tents, bring Count Olaf's troupe some potato chips or cook dinner?

35 In *The Slippery Slope*, what sort of creature arrives when the two whistles are blown: mountain lions, crows, eagles or lizards?

36 On Klaus, Violet and Sunny's first day at boarding school, who called them 'cakesniffers'?

37 In *The Ersatz Elevator*, what sort of transport does Mr Poe take a three week journey in to try to find the Quagmire children: a ship, a train, a helicopter or a hot-air balloon?

38 In *The Miserable Mill*, who did Foreman Flacutono turn out to be working for?

39 How old was Violet Baudelaire at the start of the first Lemony Snicket book?

40 In *The Hostile Hospital*, to which child did Esmé hand the jagged knife?

41 Which carnival freak was chosen to be fed to the lions: Beverley and Elliot, Colette, Madame Lulu or Hugo?

42 What item from Uncle Monty's kitchen did Violet coat her lockpick with: lard, soap, butter or washing up liquid?

43 The foreman at the Lucky Smells Lumbermill put one of the Baudelaire children in charge of the stamping machine – but which one?

44 When Violet tells the people to search for the missing children in the unfinished part of the Heimlich Hospital, does she pretend to be: Babs, Count Olaf, Hal or Esmé Squalor?

45 In *The Wide Window*, the sound of something breaking woke the three Baudelaire children up. Was it: a table, a glass window or a china vase?

46 When the children found Uncle Monty dead in the Reptile Room, how many small holes did they see below his left eye?

47 In *The Wide Window*, how many keys were on the ring of keys to Count Olaf's sailboat business?

48 In *The Vile Village*, was Hector friendly to Violet, Klaus and Sunny or was he rude and unpleasant?

49 At the carnival, how much do the freaks get paid by Madame Lulu?

50 In *The Ersatz Elevator*, did the fire tongs need to be red-hot, white-hot or yellow-hot before they were ready to be taken out of the oven?

QUIZ 5

1 Which one of the following was not a film made by Dr Sebald: *Goblins in the Garden*, *Wombats on Ice* or *Alligators in the Sewer*?

2 What was the shape of the library room in Aunt Josephine's house: a long thin rectangle, triangular, circular or oval-shaped?

3 What was the name of the region where Count Olaf drove to visit Madame Lulu: the hinterlands, the wildlands, the flatlands or the tablelands?

4 What shape were Dr Montgomery's mansion windows: square, round, triangular or oval?

5 In *The Reptile Room*, who gave a fake scream to attract Mr Poe: Count Olaf, Sunny or Violet?

6 In *The Bad Beginning*, after one of Count Olaf's henchmen switched the theatre lights off, who switched them back on?

7 Which character was pictured on the giant banner displayed at Esmé Squalor's In Auction?

8 At Prufrock School, which of the Baudelaire children was in the same class as Isadora Quagmire?

9 Violet stole items from the Prufrock School kitchen to help with her staple-making invention. Can you name any of them?

10 When the Baudelaire children are trying to escape the Heimlich Hospital, who offers to use the bungee cord first?

MISERABLY MEDIUM QUESTIONS

11 In Aunt Josephine's house, the children found a note pinned to the door of which room?

12 In *The Reptile Room*, what was the name of the harbour from which the Prospero sailed?

13 What is the name of the carnival freak who could use either arm and leg just as well: Hugo, Kevin or Palfrey?

14 What sort of sweet are Violet, Klaus and Sunny all allergic to?

15 In *The Carnivorous Carnival*, Count Olaf is going to let someone choose which Baudelaire child lives. Who is this?

16 Which book comes after *The Carnivorous Carnival*?

17 Who had arrested a man in V.F.D. village who was believed to be Count Olaf?

18 What is the surname of Klaus, Sunny and Violet's new guardians in *The Ersatz Elevator*?

19 In the fourth Lemony Snicket book, the Baudelaire children are to find their new guardian at the office of what business: a lumbermill, a bank or a sailboat rental business?

MISERABLY MEDIUM QUESTIONS

20 In *The Vile Village*, what was Count Olaf wearing around his neck and chest?

21 In *The Slippery Slope*, the man with a beard but no hair said they had just burned down which headquarters?

22 What object does Violet instruct the children to use as a battering ram to escape from the V.F.D. village jail?

23 What colour were the stone buildings of Prufrock Preparatory School?

24 What do the villains plan to use to capture all the Snow Scouts: a pit, a net, a cage or a cave?

25 What cooking item was Sunny forced to sleep in on the mountainside in *The Slippery Slope*?

26 To which building in V.F.D. did Mr Poe tell Violet, Klaus and Sunny to report when they arrived?

27 What did Klaus do with the pitcher of slime in *The Slippery Slope*?

28 In *The Bad Beginning*, whose shoulder started to bleed after being struck by the grappling hook?

MISERABLY MEDIUM QUESTIONS

29 Which one of the following items is not contained in the V.F.D. disguise kit: a sailor's suit, a safari suit, a clown's suit or a salmon suit?

30 Was the Heimlich Hospital: brand new and completed, half-finished, old and crumbling or a small house?

31 In *The Wide Window*, what did the large figure carrying all three children stand on, causing them to slip and fall?

32 At the Caligari Carnival, what shape were the lights in the ceiling of the fortune-telling tent?

33 What weapon fired by Officer Luciana hit the Quagmire children's notebooks, scattering the pages all over the place?

34 What was the name of the organization of cheerful hospital volunteers whom the children meet near the start of *The Hostile Hospital*?

35 In *The Hostile Hospital*, how many pages did the children find were remaining in the important file they opened?

MISERABLY MEDIUM QUESTIONS

36 In *The Miserable Mill*, who said to Shirley that the Baudelaire children were stupid?

37 Which one of the following was not going to be a new home for some of Uncle Monty's reptile collection: zoos, schools or retirement homes?

38 The crowds drawn to the Caligari Carnival wanted to see two things. One was violence, the other was: a light show, sloppy eating, funny clowns or cute baby bears?

39 When Klaus, Sunny and Violet were running laps at night on the Prufrock School lawn, which two children spied on them in shifts?

40 How many bottles of wine did Violet find in Stephano's opened suitcase in *The Reptile Room*?

41 The day after Gunther visited the Squalor penthouse, which king did Esmé Squalor have to meet: the King of Algeria, the King of Arizona or the King of Athens?

42 In *The Miserable Mill*, Count Olaf was to receive one half of the Baudelaire children's fortune, but which doctor was to get the other half?

43 What colour was the curly wig which Foreman Flacutono wore at the Lucky Smells Lumbermill?

44 When the Baudelaire children were holding the hot fire tongs in the Squalors' apartment, what did they use to protect their hands?

45 Count Olaf let the carnival freaks Kevin, Hugo and Colette join his gang: true or false?

46 In Dr Montgomery's house, whose room lay between Klaus' room and Violet's?

47 Is Violet Baudelaire right or left-handed?

48 One lumbermill machine was fitted with a huge, flat stone. What job did it do: tying, sawing, debarking or stamping?

49 In Lemony's unauthorized biography, which one of the following was not a named sailor in the crew of the *Prospero*: Dahl, Peck, Kalman, Randall or Eager?

50 What present had Esmé Squalor bought all the children from the In Boutique?

QUIZ 6

1 Aunt Josephine pointed out a grammatical mistake to Captain Sham on: his business card, a piece of notepaper or his store sign?

2 What was the first ride the children spotted at the Caligari Carnival?

3 At the carnival, how many freaks are living in the caravan that the Baudelaire children are shown into as their new home?

4 Which Prufrock School teacher ordered the Baudelaire children to run on the grass all through the night?

5 In V.F.D. village, the children formed a human pyramid to look at Fowl Fountain. Who stood on top?

6 The newest book added to the Squalors' library was: an auction catalogue, a book on welding or a history of Lake Lachrymose?

7 What sort of stall had Klaus, Sunny and Violet run outside their house when their parents were alive: lemonade, bric-a-brac or fresh fruit?

8 What is the name of the beach where we find the Baudelaire children at the start of *The Bad Beginning*?

9   In *The Vile Village*, who is mistakenly arrested as Count Olaf: Jacques, Hal or Hector?

10 In *The Wide Window*, what happens to Klaus when he eats peppermints?

11 Which one of the following was not a film made by Dr Sebald: *Hypnotists in the Office, Lawyers in the Jungle* or *Surgeons in the Theater*?

12 In the shack at Prufrock School, what items could the Baudelaire children use as beds?

13 At Prufrock School, what cut the rods into staple-sized pieces: Sunny's teeth, a crab's claw or a carving knife?

14 What was the name of the doctor who arrived at Uncle Monty's house wearing a white coat?

15 In *The Wide Window*, how long did Ike wait for his dinner to go down before he started swimming in the lake: 30 minutes, 45 minutes, 60 minutes or 90 minutes?

16 In *The Bad Beginning*, who had made Violet vow to look after her brother and sister as best as she could?

MISERABLY MEDIUM QUESTIONS

17 In *The Slippery Slope*, what item was inside the casserole dish instead of Sunny?

18 How did Uncle Monty die: snake poison, a book dropped on his head or a car crash?

19 When Klaus and Violet entered a cave in Mortmain Mountains, which unpleasant schoolgirl did they meet again?

20 What food did Violet and Quigley share on an ice ledge in the Mortmain Mountains when they took a rest from their climb?

21 Which one of the following items was not packed in Stephano's suitcase: a glass vial, a syringe, a long knife, a powder puff?

22 Who started crying as the lumbermill saw blade got closer and closer to cutting him?

23 How many pairs of noisy shoes did Violet make to keep away the crabs from their shack at Prufrock School?

24 In *The Unauthorized Autobiography*, there is a letter from Jacques to his brother. Whom does Jacques warn Lemony not to telephone: D, B or K?

25 When Klaus and Sunny are disguised as medical staff in Heimlich Hospital, who does the man with hooks for hands think that they are?

26 What happens to Klaus whenever he visits Dr Orwell in the town of Paltryville?

27 In *The Vile Village*, whose name was mistakenly reported as Susie in *The Daily Punctilio*?

28 How many words were in Prufrock School's motto?

29 How many people were shown in the photograph in the file the children opened at the Heimlich Hospital?

30 In *The Vile Village*, can you name either of the people Count Olaf says are accomplices to the murder of Jacques?

31 In *The Bad Beginning*, who offered to have the Baudelaire children live with them after Count Olaf's plan was discovered?

32 Where are all the V.F.D. village's inventing materials stored: in a pit, in a barn in the Town Hall or underneath the Fowl Fountain?

MISERABLY MEDIUM QUESTIONS

33 What sort of knot did Violet use to attach the carnival caravan hammocks to the door knob: the Sumac, the Devil's Tongue or the Triple Sheepshank?

34 From which floor of the Heimlich Hospital did the Baudelaire children jump?

35 Where did the children find a library at the Caligari Carnival?

36 How many lifejackets were found in the sailboat which carried the children to the Curdled Cave?

37 In *The Ersatz Elevator*, were the clothes Esmé gave the children: too small, too large or just the right fit?

38 What dangled from the flag pole in the middle of the town of Paltryville?

39 Who tells the Caligari Carnival's spectators that they are allergic to cats?

40 Which one of the following hats was not a part of the V.F.D. disguise kit: a cowboy hat, a doorman's hat, a chef's hat or a policeman's helmet?

MISERABLY MEDIUM QUESTIONS

41 How many books on crows has Klaus read in the past: none, one, three or seven?

42 In *The Reptile Room*, who called the three Baudelaire orphans 'bambini', meaning children in Italian?

43 What is the fifth book in *A Series of Unfortunate Events*?

44 What fruit did Count Olaf add to Klaus, Sunny and Violet's breakfast the day after they went to see Mr Poe?

45 What object was the first that Violet, Sunny and Klaus saw auctioned at the In Auction: a globe, a piano, a gold necklace or a vase?

46 Whose leg was broken by the lumbermill stamping machine going wrong?

47 Violet had a friend who once gave her some blueprints of an elevator as a birthday present. What was this friend's name?

48 What sort of cake had Dr Montgomery just baked as Klaus, Sunny and Violet arrived at his home?

49 In what Heimlich Hospital room does Hal store his fruit: the Library of Records, Ward 7, the ante-chamber or the reception area?

50 How many laboratories are there at the V.F.D. headquarters?

QUIZ 7

1 When the theatre lights went off, who held Sunny high up above their head to protect her?

2 How many people were in the lumbermill when Violet managed to unhypnotise Klaus: three, five or seven?

3 When Count Olaf surprised the children in the Squalors' penthouse, what sort of eyewear did he have on?

4 Jerome Squalor often had breakfast at which restaurant: the Anxious Clown, Café Salmonella, the Veritable French Diner or the In Café?

5 Which window is the only one that Aunt Josephine can bear to look at Lake Lachrymose through?

MISERABLY MEDIUM QUESTIONS

6 Who does Count Olaf insist takes his place on the plank to throw the carnival freak into the pit of lions?

7 Lot #47 at the In Auction was: a pair of ballet shoes made of chocolate, a vase full of flowers or a big, red fish?

8 What word is spelt wrongly in the second sentence of Aunt Josephine's note: unbearable, heart or dowager?

9 What group is Carmelita part of when Klaus and Violet encounter her on the mountainside in *The Slippery Slope*?

10 In *The Bad Beginning*, what was the name of the special knot Violet tied: a sheepshank, the Devil's Tongue, the Demon's Tail or a great-uncle knot?

11 What was the number of the room Violet was held in before her hospital operation: 174, 201, 922 or 1074?

12 Coach Ghengis and Carmelita Spats painted the circular running track on the school lawn: true or false?

MISERABLY MEDIUM QUESTIONS

13   In *The Ersatz Elevator*, what item of ocean decoration did the doorman glue onto the elevator doors: a dolphin, a sea urchin, a starfish or a mermaid?

14   Who does Count Olaf insist sits in the front of his car next to him as they leave the Heimlich Hospital: Esmé Squalor, Babs, the man with hooks for hands or Mr Poe?

15   In *The Reptile Room*, the Dissonant Toad could mimic human speech: true or false?

16   In the V.F.D. village, which of the following did Jacques not have: a tattoo on his ankle, dirt under his fingernails or one eyebrow?

17   When Klaus is hypnotized in *The Miserable Mill*, what name beginning with the letter 'v' does he call Violet by mistake?

18   In *The Vile Village*, who does Count Olaf say bit Jacques to death?

19   What is the name of the first play Count Olaf asks the Baudelaire children to act in?

20   What happens to Violet if she eats peppermints?

MISERABLY MEDIUM QUESTIONS

21 Who invented the Sumac knot: Count Olaf, Violet Baudelaire or Mr Poe?

22 Dr Montgomery mentioned that a certain snake must have something in its mouth or it will try to eat itself. Was this snake: the Mamba du Mal, the Doom Python or the Barbary Chewer?

23 Which one of the following was not a suggested disguise in the VFD disguise kit: chief of police, gym teacher, hot dog vendor or receptionist?

24 In *The Hostile Hospital*, what food did the storekeeper kindly give Klaus, Violet and Sunny?

25 In the shack at Prufrock School, Violet pretended something was a child's toe to lure one of the crabs. What was this?

26 Who first greeted Violet and Quigley at the end of their long mountain climb: Count Olaf, the man with hooks for hands or Sunny?

27 Where did the Baudelaire children first see the words 'Memento Mori'?

MISERABLY MEDIUM QUESTIONS

28 What was the V.F.D. Town Hall made of: black wood, red sandstone, white marble or black granite?

29 Which one of the following items was not in the boat in which Klaus, Violet and Sunny sailed: a fishing road, a treasure map, a metal bucket or a rusty spyglass?

30 Were the shops down the high street of Paltryville lacking windows, doors or roofs?

31 In *The Reptile Room*, what shiny object secured Count Olaf's suitcase?

32 When the children were moved to the Village of Fowl Devotees, which carnival member helped Count Olaf find them?

33 Does the Squirting Serpent, the Inky Newt or the Black Pen Toad leave a dark-coloured dye on your fingers if not handled correctly?

34 What was the first tool that Klaus and Violet had to use at the lumbermill: a sander, a debarker or a saw?

35 What part of the crow statue in V.F.D. village's Fowl Fountain did Sunny bite?

MISERABLY MEDIUM QUESTIONS

36 In Lemony's unauthorized autobiography, Jacques sends his brother a package secured in: a trunk, a safe or inside a leopard?

37 At Prufrock School, the Baudelaire children have to share their shack with what sort of creature?

38 Who reached the getaway car but had their hand bitten by Count Olaf's henchwoman?

39 How many clocks do Esmé and Jerome Squalor own: 142, 342, 612, or 772?

40 The strange arrivals to Count Olaf's mountain camp gave him what file?

41 The first and most important rule of V.F.D. was not to harm what creature?

42 When the Lucky Smells Lumbermill stamping machine went wrong what other machine did it damage as a result?

43 When Mr Poe and the children meet the doorman for the first time, he says two things are out of fashion. Can you name either of them?

44 Who helped Hal open the locked hospital filing cabinets when he had lost the keys?

45 Did the parents of the Quagmire children own: sapphires, rubies, diamonds or pearls?

46 When Violet was young, she won her first invention competition prize by creating an automatic device for use in cooking. What was it?

47 Which V.F.D. villager was working on inventing a self-sustaining hot air mobile home?

48 What was the decoration on the front of Madame Lulu's caravan?

49 Which gentlemen meets the Baudelaire children in most of the Lemony Snicket books and always seems to have a cold?

50 In the Baudelaire file at the hospital, Jacques Snicket was one of the people shown in the photograph: true or false?

QUIZ 8

1 At the V.F.D. village meeting, which Baudelaire child stood up to say that the arrested man was not Count Olaf?

2 In *The Hostile Hospital*, according to the note added to the file, how many survivors might there be from the fire?

3 At the In Auction, who bid for, but did not win, the giant red fish statue: Mr Poe, Jerome or Count Olaf?

4 In *The Marvelous Marriage* play, who is to play the role of the bride?

5 Stephano forced the Baudelaire children at knifepoint into a jeep, in order to leave for Hazy Harbour. Whose jeep was it?

6 A high wooden wall runs down Paltryville's one street, with a wooden gate in the middle. What is stuck to the gate to spell out the name 'Lucky Smells Lumbermill'?

7 Who created a diversion so that the Baudelaire children could steal three salt shakers from the Prufrock School canteen?

8 Officer Luciana's last harpoon hit what living creature?

9 Which elevator button did Violet press to reveal the empty elevator shaft: the up button or the down button?

10 In *The Wide Window*, who is frightened by Lake Lachrymose and many other things?

11 Uncle Monty headed off into town to get what sort of canned food for the Peru expedition?

12 In *The Hostile Hospital*, Klaus and Sunny helped push the trolley carrying Violet into the operating theatre: true or false?

13 In *The Reptile Room*, what vegetable is Sunny given to eat instead of the coconut cream cake?

14 According to *The Daily Punctilio*, who fell into the Caligari Carnival's lion pit first?

15 What object in the carnival caravan did Violet and Klaus use as a brake?

16 'Sir Isaac Newton' was one of the phrases which opened the special lock to the V.F.D. headquarters. But was this phrase the answer to the first, second or third question?

17 Was the storekeeper of the Last Chance
    General Store called: Mike, Lee, Milt or Lou?

18 Which V.F.D. village rule says 'no murdering':
    Rule #110, Rule #201, Rule #310 or Rule
    #401?

19 What normally harmless creature in Lake
    Lachrymose attacks and eats when it smells
    food on humans?

20 In *The Unauthorized Autobiography*, how many
    tickets is Lemony Snicket given to the ship,
    Prospero?

21 In *The Ersatz Elevator*, who was supposed to
    take Klaus, Violet and Sunny to the In
    Auction?

22 The children who live in the Prufrock School
    dormitory get a piece of fresh fruit on which
    day of the week?

23 In the first Lemony Snicket book, who tells
    the Baudelaire children the bad news about
    their parents?

24 Can you name either of the people who
    grabbed Violet's arms as she tried to rescue
    Charles in the Lucky Smells Lumbermill?

25 How many nights in a row did Violet, Sunny and Klaus perform S.O.R.E. sessions at Prufrock School?

26 Who laid out on the table in the Reptile Room all the evidence from Stephano's suitcase?

27 What was Count Olaf's name when he was disguised as an auctioneer at the In Auction?

28 In *The Carnivorous Carnival*, who wore a white gown with an 'I love freaks' message embroidered on it?

29 In Snicket's unauthorized autobiography, *Vampires in the Retirement Community* was a film made by Dr Sebald: true or false?

30 What did Violet plunge into the ice of the Mortmain Mountains to slow down the toboggan?

31 In the Snow Scout Alphabet Pledge, are Snow Scouts: alarming, accommodating or artistic?

32 After the sound of smashing glass, Violet found Aunt Josephine slumped in the library: true or false?

33 Which two people climbed out of the open beak of Fowl Fountain in V.F.D. village?

34 In *The Unauthorized Autobiography*, Captain S of the *Prospero* warns Lemony that enemies on board the ship are likely to be disguised as passengers or what other creature: dolphins, seagulls or sharks?

35 Who tripped Klaus up at the lumbermill, breaking his glasses for a second time?

36 On what floor of Prufrock School was Vice Principal Nero's office?

37 In *The Vile Village*, how many baskets are fitted to the self-sustaining hot air mobile home?

38 In *The Wide Window*, what sort of sweet did Violet give her brother and sister under the table whilst they were eating at the restaurant?

39 Who does Hugo ask to help put up the children's hammocks in the carnival caravan?

40 Was the Devil's Tongue knot invented by: Finnish women in the fifteenth century, Greek sailors in the fourth century or German children in the eighteenth century?

MISERABLY MEDIUM QUESTIONS

41 In *The Wide Window*, when Hurricane Herman stopped, a moonless sky was revealed: true or false?

42 On the walk from the bus stop to V.F.D., did Sunny: get sunburned, fall asleep or twist her ankle?

43 The Baudelaire orphans' new guardian and owner of the Lucky Smells Lumbermill is known by what word beginning with 's'?

44 While the Baudelaire children attended Prufrock School, they were forced to live in a shack with walls of what colour?

45 In the Caligari Carnival fortune-telling tent, what fell off the table and shattered?

46 In *The Slippery Slope*, after Violet and Quigley reached the top of the mountain, what did they hide underneath?

47 What food item from Prufrock School did Violet use as a glue to build her staple-making machine?

48 Which newspaper published the obituary of Lemony Snicket?

49   In *The Reptile Room*, what part of Violet's body was sore from the car crash: her leg, her hand, her shoulder or her back?

50   What were Klaus and Violet to do with the paper clips that came with the papers down the information chute at Heimlich Hospital?

QUIZ 9

1   Which residents of V.F.D. village were required to bring torches to the burning at the stake: the uptown or downtown residents?

2   Which of these is correct: Aunt Josephine is a widow, Aunt Josephine has never married or Aunt Josephine was married to Mr Poe?

3   Was Lot #14 at the In Auction: an atlas, an enormous globe or a grand piano?

4   When the Baudelaire children were cleaning the fountain in V.F.D. village, what sound drowned out Duncan and Isadora's cries for help?

5   According to Count Olaf, who wrote the play, *The Marvelous Marriage*?

MISERABLY MEDIUM QUESTIONS

6 Despite his poor eyesight, Hal always reads *The Daily Punctilio* from cover to cover: true or false?

7 Which member of Count Olaf's gang fell into the lion pit: one of the two white-faced ladies, the bald man, the man with hooks for hands or Esmé Squalor?

8 When the Baudelaire children receive news of the death of their parents, at whose house are they to stay for a short time?

9 To whom did the Lucky Smells Lumbermill owner threaten to hand over the children if they continued to be bad workers: the police, Shirley or Mr Poe?

10 What shape is the building at the far end of the street from the Lucky Smells Lumbermill?

11 What was the name of Dr Montgomery's assistant who resigned: Stephano, Gustav or Lucafont?

12 According to Jerome, what was the quickest way to get down from the penthouse to the ground floor?

MISERABLY MEDIUM QUESTIONS

13 In *The Miserable Mill*, Mr Poe's promotion meant that he was Vice President in charge of: loans, debts, coins or paper clips?

14 Who captured Violet as she tried to rescue Sunny from Count Olaf's tower: the women with white faces, Mr Poe, or the man with hooks for hands?

15 What had the V.F.D. village Council of Elders instructed Hector to do with all the books that broke Rule #108?

16 The waters of the Stricken Stream separated Klaus, Violet and Sunny from whom?

17 When Charles worked at the Lucky Smells Lumbermill, what colour was the vest that he wore?

18 At Prufrock School, what cutlery item did Violet use to bend over pieces of wire so that they turned into staples?

19 Whose hand did Sunny bite in the Lucky Smells Lumbermill?

20 In *The Reptile Room*, which snake both poisons its victims and strangles them, leaving them dark all over with bruises?

MISERABLY MEDIUM QUESTIONS

21 What was Klaus supposed to be measuring when he fell asleep in class at Prufrock School and got a test mark of zero?

22 In Stephano's suitcase there was a glass vial. What did the label on the side of it say?

23 At the start of *The Carnivorous Carnival*, how do the Baudelaire children try to contact Mr Poe?

24 According to Lemony Snicket's unauthorized autobiography, *Chiropodists on Mars* was a film made by Dr Sebald: true or false?

25 When Sunny Baudelaire eats a peppermint, does her tongue swell up, does she get a rash or do both things happen?

26 Which one of the following was not a feature on the *Prospero* ship: the Black Rapids Deck, the Crystal Ballroom or the White Jacket Lounge?

27 On the children's first visit to the V.F.D. Town Hall, one woman was not wearing the same hat as everyone else in the building. What sort of hat was she wearing?

28 At the In Auction, who successfully bid for the giant red fish statue: Mr Poe, the doorman, Count Olaf or Jerome Squalor?

29 What was the name of the stream in the Mortmain Mountains whose source was believed to be close to the V.F.D. headquarters?

30 The two mysterious visitors to Count Olaf's mountain camp had searched for days without finding which item?

31 Who burst into tears in the carnival's fortune-telling tent after the Baudelaire children had called her a fraud?

32 How many rows of sharp teeth do the Lachrymose Leeches have: two, four, six or eight?

33 The operation to be performed on Violet in Heimlich Hospital was a world's first: true or false?

34 At Prufrock School, children who were late to meals had what taken away from them: cups and bowls, knives and forks or food?

35 In *The Vile Village*, who turned out to be Count Olaf's girlfriend?

36 Which two of the following were features on the atlas map of Lake Lachrymose: Rancorous Rocks, Raven's Reef, Wicked Whirlpool, Hellfire Island?

37 In the Snow Scout Alphabet Pledge, are Snow Scouts: wonderful, warmhearted or wholesome?

38 What was the name of Prufrock School's new gym teacher?

39 According to Lemony Snicket, how many burglars throughout history specialised in stealing rope: one, five, nine or 11?

40 In *The Reptile Room*, the jeep containing Stephano and the children crashed into whose car?

41 In *The Hostile Hospital*, who wore a coat which had a secret pocket in which a pocket dictionary was often stored: Klaus, the Baudelaire children's mother or Count Olaf?

42 According to the *Unauthorized Autobiography*, where was Lemony Snicket born: in a hospital, in a castle dungeon or on a farm?

43 In *The Carnivorous Carnival*, what object of Count Olaf's did the children use to disguise Sunny as a wolf creature?

44 Who had read the *Encyclopedia Hypnotica* a year before working in the Lucky Smells Lumbermill?

45 Which V.F.D. villager always goes very quiet in the presence of the Council of Elders?

46 At the carnival, who does Esmé want to throw into the pit of lions instead of the freaks?

47 Klaus says Prufrock School's motto is written in what language?

48 Which one of the following items was not part of the burned remains of the V.F.D. headquarters: an ice cream scoop, a ski pole, a refrigerator or a trombone?

49 After Aunt Josephine disappeared, who called Mr Poe?

50 In *The Hostile Hospital*, what colour was the small van with V.F.D. written on its side?

QUIZ 10

1 Who was the first person that Klaus called
'a cakesniffer': Carmelita, Coach Ghengis or
Isadora?

2 Who wrote a two-hundred page book to
Lemony Snicket explaining why she could
not marry him?

3 In the village of V.F.D., the uptown jail is
opposite what landmark?

4 What normal facial feature did Stephano not
have?

5 When Violet and Klaus were younger, what
contest did they go to see their Uncle Elwyn
enter?

6 Whose plastic identity card did Stephano pack
in his suitcase?

7 In the test at Prufrock School, which of the
following did Klaus not have to know the
measurements of: a yellow book, a tube sock,
a casserole dish or a chicken breast?

8 What was the name of the café that Lemony
Snicket sat in as he read his own obituary:
the Anxious Clown, Café Salmonella or
Café Kafka?

9 What is the name of the hurricane the taxi driver says will hit Lake Lachrymose?

10 In which building had Hector built a secret library?

11 According to Klaus, what does the Prufrock School motto mean in English?

12 In what district of the city was Café Salmonella located?

13 To which South American country does Dr Montgomery say he will take the Baudelaire children on their first snake expedition?

14 Who was taken to hospital in an ambulance after a lumbermill accident: Phil, Klaus, Foreman Flacutono or Charles?

15 What did Coach Ghengis wear around his neck?

16 A Snow Scout in a sweater led Klaus and Violet to the V.F.D. headquarters. What was this Snow Scout's name?

17 In *The Slippery Slope*, what meal did Sunny plan to make Count Olaf's troupe to celebrate False Spring?

MISERABLY MEDIUM QUESTIONS

18 Which member of the Caligari Carnival had a disguise kit similar to Count Olaf's?

19 Who discovered the children in the hospital's Library of Records at night: Count Olaf, Babs, Esmé Squalor or Hal?

20 When the children arrived at the penthouse, what sort of drink did Jerome Squalor offer them: buttermilk, parsley soda, an aqueous martini or carrot juice?

21 What musical instrument did Hugo the carnival freak play some afternoons: ukulele, guitar, banjo or violin?

22 What was the name of the meeting group taking place in the V.F.D. Town Hall on the children's arrival?

23 Who said that she did not have enough freaks for her House of Freaks?

24 How were Sunny, Violet and Klaus' parents killed: by robbers, in a fire, in an earthquake or by a flood?

25 How many police detectives were sent to investigate the murder at the Lucky Smells Lumbermill?

MISERABLY MEDIUM QUESTIONS

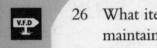

26 What item of Violet's does Count Olaf maintain he found in the V.F.D. village jail in which Jacques was imprisoned?

27 In *The Miserable Mill*, what emerged from Dr Orwell's cane when the red jewel was pressed?

28 In *The Carnivorous Carnival*, who becomes envious of Count Olaf buying Madame Lulu presents?

29 What did the sign in front of the Curdled Cave indicate?

30 In whose house were Duncan and Isadora hidden in after they had been smuggled away from the In Auction?

31 How many books did Klaus use to discover the coded message in Aunt Josephine's note: one, two or three?

32 What substance did Uncle Monty keep in test tubes: snakes' venom, lizards' claws, the tongues of frogs or samples of rotten eggs?

33 Who kept on saying 'Yes, sir' to Violet when they were in the lumbermill workers' dormitory?

34 What was painted on the knob of the door in Count Olaf's tower?

35 Did Stephano arrive at Dr Montgomery's house by: train, taxi, motorbike or helicopter?

36 What was written on the side of the cardboard box that was Lot #50 in the In Auction?

37 Violet and Klaus explained to Mr Poe that they thought Aunt Josephine's note was a forgery: true or false?

38 Which one of Count Olaf's henchmen is put in charge of the carnival's House of Freaks?

39 The man by the V.F.D. van outside the Last Chance General Store held what musical instrument in his hand?

40 What is Madame Lulu's real first name?

41 In which files in the Heimlich Hospital did Hal say there was information about the children?

42 In *The Miserable Mill*, what fruit was Charles eating when he first met Klaus, Sunny and Violet?

43 In *The Ersatz Elevator*, what item of clothing did Sunny collect for the children to use as rope?

44 In *The Hostile Hospital*, Hal turned out to be a private detective hired by Mr Poe: true or false?

45 What flavour pudding did Violet, Klaus and Sunny serve Count Olaf and his theatre troupe after the pasta and puttanesca sauce?

46 What word stands for X in the Snow Scouts' Alphabet Pledge?

47 Who told Mr Poe that Dr Montgomery was dead?

48 In Esmé Squalor's In Auction catalogue, what three letters were listed as Lot #50?

49 In Lemony Snicket's unauthorized autobiography, what is the first name of the lady who was the executor of Dr Sebald's estate: Sally, Gwendoline, Jackie or Hermione?

50 In *The Slippery Slope*, who was going to be crowned False Spring Queen by the Snow Scouts?

QUIZ 11

1 What was the Baudelaire children's first meal at Prufrock Preparatory School: fried eggs, porridge, lasagne or roast beef?

2 What colour was the jewel in the centre of Coach Ghengis' headwear?

3 Which of the following was one of the books Klaus used to discover his Aunt's secret message: *The Essential Adjectives Manual*, *Handbook for Advanced Apostrophe Use*, *The Ultimate Guide to Capital Letters*?

4 Who did the Baudelaire children tell first of Count Olaf's plot to smuggle the Quagmire children out of the city?

5 In *The Carnivorous Carnival*, what did the man with hooks for hands use as a whip: strips of bacon, pasta or a piece of rope?

6 How was the 200 page book sent to Lemony Snicket: by post, by courier, by aircraft or by carrier pigeons?

7 What were the vases on the tables of Café Salmonella filled with instead of flowers?

8 When the Baudelaire children first met Vice Principal Nero, what creature decorated his tie?

9   In Snicket's unauthorized autobiography, whose fan club outbid others in an auction for the Mamba du Mal snake?

10   At the In Auction, who did Klaus ask to bid on Lot #50 on behalf of him and his sisters?

11   In *The Bad Beginning*, according to Mr Poe, what is the name of the distant relative Sunny, Violet and Klaus are to go to live with?

12   What is the full name of Count Olaf's enemy, Jacques?

13   According to Lulu's map, what was located next to Plath Pass: a campground, a bear hibernating site or a petrol station?

14   From where did the children get items to disguise themselves to enter the Caligari Carnival?

15   What was Mr Poe bringing to Uncle Monty's mansion when he crashed into the jeep?

16   What was the name, beginning with the letter 'n', of the biggest tree Sunny, Klaus and Violet had ever seen?

17 In *The Reptile Room*, Count Olaf threatened to cut off one of the toes of which of the Baudelaire children?

18 What present did Esmé Squalor give Kevin the carnival freak so that he could tie one hand behind his back and be left-handed?

19 Esmé Squalor was wearing the exact same kind of suit as her husband when the children first met her: true or false?

20 Who slept in the unfinished part of Heimlich Hospital after their day's work?

21 What did Aunt Josephine throw through the Wide Window to break it: a brick, a footstool, the telephone or a coffee table?

22 Which member of Klaus' family had in the past taken him fishing, after warning him that it was one of the most boring activities in the world?

23 Mr Remora stopped eating a banana to say to the Vice Principal of Prufrock School that Violet was a good student. Was this his fifth, eighth or eleventh banana?

24 What mountain feature did Klaus and Violet follow to find their way through the Mortmain Mountains straight after the carnival caravan crashed?

25 What was the name of the doctor, Klaus, Violet and Sunny met in the eye-shaped building in Paltryville?

26 What colour was the door of Aunt Josephine's house?

27 One of Count Olaf's theatre troupe has: false hands, hooks for hands or three hands?

28 What did Carmelita ask for every time she delivered a message to Klaus, Violet and Sunny at Prufrock School?

29 The penthouse Jerome Squalor bought was on what street?

30 In *The Slippery Slope*, what colour were the uniforms worn by the Snow Scouts?

31 According to Lemony Snicket's newspaper column, the Nancarrow Theater allows the audience to bring live sheep with them on what night of the week?

MISERABLY MEDIUM QUESTIONS

32   What is written on the nameplate on the desk in the lumbermill chief's office?

33   Who called the Herpetological Society to tell them the bad news about Dr Montgomery?

34   In *The Reptile Room*, what make-up item had Count Olaf used to cover up the tattoo on his ankle?

35   What did Mr Poe use to get a sample of Aunt Josephine's handwriting: a diary, a shopping list or a note to the milkman?

36   After Quigley walked through the secret passageway from his burned-down home, where did he end up?

37   What is the motto of the Volunteers Fighting Disease?

38   In his unauthorized autobiography, what is the name of the boat Lemony Snicket boards after reading about his own death?

39   While the Baudelaire children are at the Lucky Smells Lumbermill, they never see the face of their new guardian because it is hidden by smoke from what?

40 Did the sailor the children encountered in *The Wide Window* have: a left wooden leg, a right wooden leg or two wooden legs?

41 In *The Hostile Hospital* who carried a handbag in the shape of an eye and wore a fur coat?

42 What smell followed travellers along Lousy Lane, the smell of: garlic, cow manure or horseradish?

43 In *The Ersatz Elevator*, the extension cords and other items were tied together to form a rope using what type of knot?

44 When the Baudelaire children took off their disguises and revealed themselves to Madame Lulu at the carnival, where were they standing?

45 Who said their longest ever sentence to Violet whilst Violet was underneath a car in *The Slippery Slope*?

46 Mattathias announced over the hospital intercom that a 14-year-old girl was to have an operation in: half an hour, an hour, two hours or three hours?

47 After Violet was wheeled into the operating theatre at Heimlich Hospital, what did all the spectators do?

48 Who spent the night underneath the Nevermore Tree trying to spot the person leaving the poems as notes?

49 In *The Bad Beginning*, what did the man with no hands use to contact Count Olaf to tell him Violet had tried to rescue Sunny?

50 All the people inside the V.F.D. Town Hall were wearing what item of clothing?

QUIZ 12

1 The night that the children dined with Jerome at Café Salmonella, what was not on the menu: salmon salad, salmon ravioli, salmon fritters or salmon ice cream?

2 Who irons the lumbermill owner's shirts and cooks him omelettes: Hal, Charles or Foreman Flacutono?

3 In *The Wide Window*, who did Violet spot at the grocery store in a sailor's disguise?

MISERABLY MEDIUM QUESTIONS

4   In *The Reptile Room*, who wiped away the powder on Count Olaf's ankle to discover his tattoo?

5   In *The Vile Village*, what item of Klaus' does Count Olaf say he found near the scene of the murder: a book on psychology, a lens from a pair of glasses or a notebook?

6   How many of Count Olaf's henchmen stood with Klaus and Sunny in the operating theatre just before the surgery was supposed to start?

7   In *The Bad Beginning*, what is the name of the woman who lives next door to Count Olaf?

8   Who discovered Quigley Quagmire at Dr Montgomery's house?

9   Who bought Klaus, Sunny and Violet really ugly clothing shortly after the death of their parents?

10 The librarian at the Prufrock Preparatory School was: a young woman, an old man, a middle-aged woman or a talking dog?

11 What was the name of the V.F.D. village's new Chief of Police?

MISERABLY MEDIUM QUESTIONS

12 When Aunt Josephine went sailing on the boat, how many lifejackets did she wear?

13 What were children supposed to give Vice Principal Nero if they missed one of his violin concerts?

14 What is the name of the official representative of Lemony Snicket: Brett Helquist, Daniel Handler, Klaus Simmons or Jacques Snicket?

15 Who pushed Klaus, Sunny and Violet down the elevator shaft?

16 *The World Is Quiet Here* was a play written by: Ned H. Rirger, Al Funcoot or the Duchess of Winnipeg?

17 What would you find at 141 Dark Avenue: the Veritable French Diner, the Nancarrow Theater, the Anxious Clown café or the Daedalus Dock?

18 What was the name of the lady V.F.D. villager who led the chant of 'Burn the orphans': Mrs Plumpton, Mrs Morrow or Mrs Strauss?

19 How many tufts of hair did Vice Principal Nero have tied in little pigtails on his head?

MISERABLY MEDIUM QUESTIONS

20　According to Violet, what was wrong with the pipes on Hector's self-sustaining mobile home: they were made of the wrong material, they were ill-fitting, or they were not long enough?

21　Who tried to use chewing gum to stop the lumbermill saw machine from killing Charles?

22　What item did not come with the children's first meal at Prufrock School: green salad, boiled cabbage or garlic bread?

23　What was the name of the valley on Madame Lulu's map which spelled V.F.D.?

24　In *The Hostile Hospital*, who says children should not read files but happy books instead?

25　According to Madame Lulu, what mountain range contains one of the last surviving headquarters of the V.F.D.?

26　In *The Austere Academy*, what colour were the little hearts daubed on the walls of the Baudelaire children's shack: pink, red or white?

27　How long did Mr Poe tell the children it would take for them to be adopted by Captain Sham: the rest of the day, the rest of the week or the rest of the month?

MISERABLY MEDIUM QUESTIONS

28 Which room in Dr Montgomery's house had glass walls and a glass ceiling?

29 What colour suit was worn by the lumbermill boss known as 'Sir'?

30 Who asked Mr Poe if they could have a bank loan in order to buy Lot #50 at the In Auction?

31 What item was strapped to the roof of Uncle Monty's jeep when he returned to his house?

32 What word was written on the Snow Scouts' headband: Chilled, Brr! or Scout?

33 In *The Carnivorous Carnival*, what, beginning with the letter 'f', did the children disguise themselves as?

34 In which auction item were Duncan and Isadora Quagmire hidden?

35 Who was the first of the freaks to perform on the children's first working day at the carnival?

36 Who said that missing athletics to study for exams was good time management: Mr Remora, Vice Principal Nero or Klaus Baudelaire?

MISERABLY MEDIUM QUESTIONS

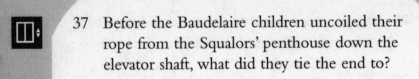

37 Before the Baudelaire children uncoiled their rope from the Squalors' penthouse down the elevator shaft, what did they tie the end to?

38 Does Esmé Squalor bring Colette the contortionist: a big dress, a large rubber band or a black overcoat as a present?

39 Aunt Josephine's house was perched on a steep hill overlooking what lake?

40 In *The Slippery Slope*, what item of clothing did Klaus wear turned inside-out?

41 Where did the Baudelaire children find their aunt's books about Lake Lachrymose?

42 In *The Reptile Room*, who was asked to cause a distraction and thought about the Trojan horse used in an ancient war?

43 In *The Slippery Slope*, who shone a torch to help guide Violet and Quigley in their climb down the icy slope?

44 In *The Miserable Mill*, the dormitory where the Baudelaire children were to live lay between the Lucky Smells Lumbermill and what other building?

MISERABLY MEDIUM QUESTIONS

45 What type of jewel was in the short poem Hector showed the children the first day they arrived in V.F.D.?

46 In *The Miserable Mill*, who wore black boots and carried a black cane with a bright red jewel on its top?

47 Were all the volunteers in the V.F.D. van going towards the hospital: miserable, angry, cheerful or sleeping?

48 What had Count Olaf grown as part of his disguise as Stephano?

49 Can you name either of Esmé Squalor's middle names, both of which start with the letter 'g'?

50 What sort of cupboard did Sunny and Klaus hide in so that they could read the Heimlich Hospital patients list?

QUIZ 13

1 How many books did Violet, Sunny and Klaus' parents have in their house: no books, a small number of books or a large library?

MISERABLY MEDIUM QUESTIONS

2 As Jerome and the children came back from Café Salmonella, what kind of decorating did the doorman say was in: jungle, ocean or desert?

3 In *The Miserable Mill*, with what did Sunny fight Dr Orwell's sword?

4 Who was summoned to the surgical ward by Mattathias over the intercom: Dr Funcoot, Dr Flacutono, Dr Doping or Dr Gram?

5 Quigley spied a signal made in green smoke coming from the top of what mountain feature?

6 The Chief of Police before Luciana became ill from swallowing: poison, a seagull, a box of thumbtacks or a toad?

7 Shortly into Violet and Klaus' journey through the Mortmain Mountains, they encountered a swarm of what insect?

8 Who does Violet think wrote the first poem the children see on their arrival in V.F.D.?

9 In *The Reptile Room*, what item was used to wipe away the powder on Count Olaf's ankle to find the tattoo?

MISERABLY MEDIUM QUESTIONS

10 How long did it take for the children to climb down to the bottom of the elevator shaft: over an hour, over three hours, over five hours or over nine hours?

11 Who won the auction for Lot #50: Mr Poe, Jerome Squalor, Sunny Baudelaire or Count Olaf?

12 Who turned up at Uncle Monty's house in a small grey car?

13 In *The Hostile Hospital*, what sort of implement was fitted into the heels of Esmé Squalor's shoes making it difficult for her to run?

14 What advanced machine was in the office of the Vice Principal of Prufrock School?

15 Duncan and Isadora tied their notes containing poems to what creature?

16 Which Prufrock School teacher was later arrested for bank robbery?

17 Which one of the following things could not be found under Aunt Josephine's bed: a framed photo of her husband, a stove or ugly socks?

18 What false name did Violet give to the volunteers in the V.F.D. van: Veronica, Sally, Verona or Susie?

19 In *The Bad Beginning*, who did Klaus confront in the kitchen with a book called Nuptial Law?

20 Who had insisted that a library was created for the workers at the Lucky Smells Lumbermill?

21 In *The Hostile Hospital*, the man with hooks for hands introduced himself as Dr Tocuna: true or false?

22 What item was given to Klaus and Violet by the Snow Scouts to protect them from snow gnats?

23 What object broke the Baudelaire children's fall down the elevator shaft?

24 What colour was Violet's suitcase: grey, red, brown or blue?

25 When very fresh dill is found inside a certain item it means that a secret message is there too. What is this item?

26 What plant had grown all over the carts on the Caligari Carnival's rollercoaster?

MISERABLY MEDIUM QUESTIONS

27 When a Mamba du Mal says, 'Summer is' does it mean: 'Hide', 'Enemies are nearby' or 'The coast is clear'?

28 The three Baudelaire children had missed nine violin concerts but how many bags of sweets did Vice Principal Nero reckon they owed him: 27, 29 or 31?

29 How much was it going to cost the Baudelaire orphans to stay at the lumbermill?

30 What was the first name of Dr Orwell's receptionist?

31 What weapon did Stephano produce to threaten Violet not to tell Uncle Monty about his real identity?

32 What was the only item of furniture in the Deluxe Cell in V.F.D. village?

33 On their second day at work in Heimlich Hospital, who uses the intercom system to make an announcement: Mr Poe, Babs, Count Olaf or Hal?

34 Rule #19 at V.F.D. village says that pens can only be made out of what?

35 In *The Austere Academy*, who doubly-expelled Sunny, Klaus and Violet?

36 Who wrote to Professor Patton to dispute the accuracy of the folk song, *The Little Snicket Lad*?

37 In *The Ersatz Elevator*, who was the city's sixth most important financial advisor?

38 When the children sailed through the territory of the Lachrymose Leeches, what did they say was the last thing they had eaten?

39 What colour was the lacy dress that Violet had to wear to take part in the play with Count Olaf's theatre troupe?

40 In *The Carnivorous Carnival*, which two children disguised themselves as a two-headed freak?

41 What is the name of Lemony Snicket's brother, who writes to Jerome Squalor pleading with him to not marry Esmé?

42 What word beginning with the letter 's' did Olivia use to describe a big fight between the members of the V.F.D.: standoff, schism or struggle?

MISERABLY MEDIUM QUESTIONS

43 Who does Violet ask to keep an eye on Klaus whilst she and Sunny visit the lumbermill boss?

44 What is carved into the front door of Count Olaf's house?

45 Which boy invited the Baudelaire children to sit at his table in the Prufrock School cafeteria?

46 What heating item does Aunt Josephine warn the children never to switch on?

47 After the children's first performance at the carnival, what sort of hot drink did Hugo make?

48 What was the name of the restaurant where the children and Mr Poe were to meet Captain Sham?

49 Who was fired after giving a bad review to the play, *One Last Warning to Those Who Try to Stand in My Way*?

50 Where did Count Olaf and his henchpeople plan to head once the carnival had burned down?

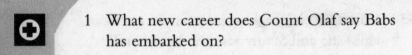

1 What new career does Count Olaf say Babs has embarked on?

2 Who considers themselves to be the finest violinist in the world: Vice Principal Nero, Jerome Squalor or Al Funcoot?

3 In *The Bad Beginning*, who does Count Olaf plan to marry to gain control of the Baudelaire fortune?

4 To act in the play, what did Klaus have to wear: a clown's suit, a sailor's suit, a dinner suit or a soldier's uniform?

5 In the Library of Records, what did Esmé Squalor start toppling over, which fell like dominoes?

6 What colour was Klaus' suitcase: beige, black, grey or white?

7 What sort of books did Klaus read all night before the morning of Jacques' execution in V.F.D. village?

8 Can you name either of the teachers that Vice Principal Nero says have been teaching at Prufrock School for more than 47 years?

MISERABLY MEDIUM QUESTIONS

9 In *The Slippery Slope*, who did the snow gnats sting first?

10 Who volunteered to work on Uncle Monty's snake traps: Violet, Klaus or Mr Poe?

11 How many bedrooms are there in the Squalors' penthouse apartment: 21, 31, 51 or 71?

12 What fruit had Aunt Josephine eaten just before the children arrived at Curdled Cave?

13 What did the Vice Principal insist Klaus, Sunny and Violet do on their first meeting: applaud, kneel down or cheer?

14 What is the name of the queen in the story Lemony Snicket writes in the middle of *The Carnivorous Carnival*?

15 What creature can be trained to communicate in coded English: crickets, bats, frogs or spiders?

16 What shape balloons do the Volunteers Fighting Disease give out to patients?

17 Has Lemony Snicket ever visited the Caligari Carnival?

18 On Count Olaf's living room wall was the stuffed head of what jungle animal?

19 What was the name of the waiter who served the Baudelaire children at the Anxious Clown eating place?

20 Which adult visitor to Dr Montgomery's house had very stiff hands?

21 In *The Vile Village*, what flew above the children as the angry mob got close to them?

22 What was the name of the Editor-in-Chief of *The Daily Punctilio* who fired Lemony Snicket?

23 Dr Lucafont said he found the venom of a certain snake in the blood of Uncle Monty. What snake was it?

24 What is the name of the tree in V.F.D. village that the crows roost in at night?

25 In *The Slippery Slope*, what was the first name of the adult with the Snow Scouts?

26 At the lumbermill, who offered his help to the Baudelaire children by giving them raisins for their lunch the next day?

27 What is Jerome Squalor's highest bid on Lot #50: 180, 200, 204 or 300?

28 What was the name of the detective reported in *The Daily Punctilio* who was present at the site of the burnt-down Valorous Farms Dairy: Smith, Jones, Jackson or Smithjones?

29 A friend of Madame Lulu's had originally trained the lions to smell what?

30 How many bedrooms did Aunt Josephine give Klaus, Sunny and Violet?

31 In Uncle Monty's house, who slept in their new room in a chair?

32 When Klaus and Sunny hid in the Heimlich Hospital supply cupboard, Klaus asked Sunny to open a can of what foodstuff?

33 Who said the mark on Madame Lulu's map was a coded stain?

34 How many of the Baudelaire children does Count Olaf say will be burned at the stake?

35 Vice Principal Nero says Sunny, Violet and Klaus owe Carmelita Spats ten pairs of what item of jewellery?

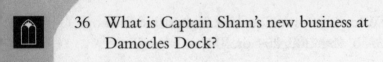

36 What is Captain Sham's new business at Damocles Dock?

37 Who had received a biography of a poet called Ogden Nash for their seventh birthday?

38 Who was Esmé Squalor's former acting teacher?

39 What part of the body is removed in a cranioectomy?

40 What is Sunny's disguise at Madame Lulu's House of Freaks?

41 In *The Miserable Mill*, who was Count Olaf disguised as: Dr Orwell, Shirley, Foreman Flacutono or Charles?

42 In *The Slippery Slope*, who set light to some weeds to both cook the salmon and send a signal?

43 What lumbermill tool did Klaus use to cast chewing gum at the saw mill: a saw, a debarker or an axe?

44 In *The Slippery Slope*, what two words were written in pencil on *The Garden of Proserpine* poem read by the children?

MISERABLY MEDIUM QUESTIONS

45 What do the Baudelaire orphans have for lunch at the Lucky Smells Lumbermill?

46 What colour is Duncan Quagmire's notebook?

47 In *The Ersatz Elevator*, what metal object did the children find at the bottom of the elevator shaft?

48 What was the place spelled out in the secret message in Aunt Josephine's note?

49 The Lucky Smells Lumbermill's library consisted of how many books?

50 Which adult appeared at the shack at Prufrock School carrying lots of paper bags of sweets?

QUIZ 15

1 In *The Miserable Mill*, who held Sunny in place with their foot as they tried to kill her?

2 In *The Slippery Slope*, the five olives in the fridge code meant that the meeting of the volunteers would take place on what day of the week?

MISERABLY MEDIUM QUESTIONS

3 In *The Hostile Hospital*, Klaus, pretending to be Dr Tocuna, first stalled the operation by telling the history of what sort of tool?

4 The tower on top of Count Olaf's house had how many windows?

5 What is the name of Babs' replacement as Head of Human Resources at Heimlich Hospital?

6 According to Esmé Squalor, what type of soda replaced aqueous martinis as the in drink?

7 What job did the Vice Principal say Sunny would have to do at Prufrock School?

8 Was Lemony Snicket brought up at: Valiant Farms Dairy, Waterfall Farms Dairy or Valorous Farms Dairy?

9 On the night of Stephano's arrival, what meal did he, the Baudelaire children and Uncle Monty eat: stroganoff, curry, roast beef or spaghetti?

10 What metal item do all the workers in the Prufrock School cafeteria wear?

MISERABLY MEDIUM QUESTIONS

11 What device did Hector release for the children to climb into his flying home?

12 The Reptile Room was lined with how many neat rows of cages?

13 Who says that Aunt Josephine is one of his closest friends, even though he only met her the day before?

14 In *The Vile Village*, whose body did the Baudelaire children see covered in a white sheet?

15 In *The Ersatz Elevator*, what paper item did the cardboard box of Lot #50 contain?

16 In *The Hostile Hospital*, what is the name of the hospital the volunteers first arrive at?

17 In *The Austere Academy*, who offered to home-school Sunny, Klaus and Violet if they failed their exams and were expelled?

18 Klaus, Violet and Sunny's knocking on the door of the lumbermill dormitory was the first time someone had knocked there for: a year, 4 years, 10 years or 14 years?

MISERABLY MEDIUM QUESTIONS

19 In the land ruled by Queen Debbie, described by Lemony Snicket in *The Carnivorous Carnival*, what sort of creature sang and did all the chores?

20 Which one of the following was not in the index of *A Lachrymose Atlas*: Clouded Peak, Carp Cove, Condiment Bay or Chartreuse Island?

21 Who believes that the Mamba du Mal got out of its cage, bit Uncle Monty and then locked itself back up in its cage?

22 In the village of V.F.D., who is to be responsible for the Baudelaire children's clothes, food and housing?

23 Violet built an ice climbing device using the strings of what musical instrument?

24 What facial feature did Aunt Josephine's mother-in-law have only one of: teeth, ears or eyes?

25 Who released the Incredibly Deadly Viper to cause a scene with Mr Poe and the other adults?

26 What one item of food does Officer Luciana bring to the children in the V.F.D. jail?

27 What reason did Coach Ghengis give for not taking off his turban: his head smelled bad, religious convictions or it was glued on?

28 Violet's first snow gnat sting was on what part of her body?

29 In *The Bad Beginning*, to whom does Violet suggest that they alter their lines in the play?

30 Was Count Olaf: small and hunched, tall and thin, or round and fat?

31 Who bit Dr Lucafont's hand in *The Reptile Room*?

32 Who sends the V.F.D. a coded message in the film, *Werewolves in the Rain*: Jacques Snicket, Mr Poe, Madame Lulu or Dr Sebald?

33 What present did Aunt Josephine buy Klaus?

34 Who announced that the Caligari Carnival show featuring a freak being fed to the lions was just starting?

MISERABLY MEDIUM QUESTIONS

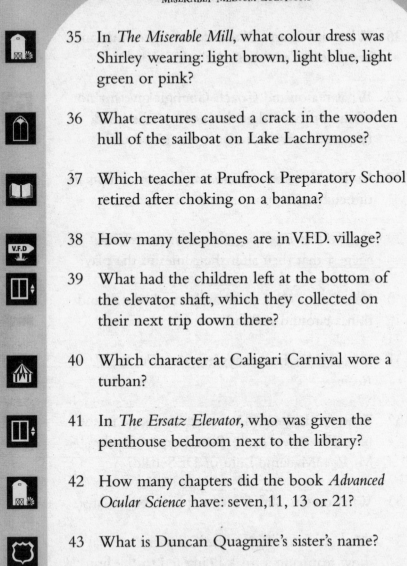

35 In *The Miserable Mill*, what colour dress was Shirley wearing: light brown, light blue, light green or pink?

36 What creatures caused a crack in the wooden hull of the sailboat on Lake Lachrymose?

37 Which teacher at Prufrock Preparatory School retired after choking on a banana?

38 How many telephones are in V.F.D. village?

39 What had the children left at the bottom of the elevator shaft, which they collected on their next trip down there?

40 Which character at Caligari Carnival wore a turban?

41 In *The Ersatz Elevator*, who was given the penthouse bedroom next to the library?

42 How many chapters did the book *Advanced Ocular Science* have: seven, 11, 13 or 21?

43 What is Duncan Quagmire's sister's name?

44 Beginning with the letter 'm', what do Snow Scouts eat after story time until they feel almost sick?

MISERABLY MEDIUM QUESTIONS

45 What do Count Olaf and Esmé do to the carnival to destroy all the evidence?

46 In *The Hostile Hospital*, what blocked the information chute, splitting up Violet from her brother and sister?

47 In *The Carnivorous Carnival*, who interrupts the children's first meeting with Olivia demanding wine?

48 Who turned out to be trapped in a cage in the building at 667 Dark Avenue?

49 What does Foreman Flacutono repeatedly mistake the three Baudelaire children for: mice, midgets or circus dwarves?

50 What was the name of the eating place which supplied the food for Esmé's wedding: Bistro Botulism, the Rancid Turbot, Café Salmonella or the Dirty Diner?

QUIZ 16

1 Which Baudelaire child was scheduled for a cranioectomy operation?

MISERABLY MEDIUM QUESTIONS

 2 Who was Violet's class teacher at Prufrock Preparatory School?

 3 In *The Wide Window*, can you name the two people who rowed the sailboat oars?

 4 In *The Austere Academy*, where were some of Count Olaf's henchmen and women working all the time?

 5 The ruin of Heimlich Hospital is covered with a type of ivy called: candlewick, kylie, kudzu or canton?

 6 What sort of glass object hung around Madame Lulu's neck?

 7 What does Captain Sham say chewed away his left leg?

 8 In *The Ersatz Elevator*, what sort of inventing furniture was in Violet's bedroom?

 9 Where had Hector found the poem the children believed was written by Isadora?

 10 What object had both Duncan and Isadora Quagmire managed to keep, despite their kidnap by Count Olaf?

MISERABLY MEDIUM QUESTIONS

11 According to a book Klaus had read, what drives snow gnats away?

12 What item did Violet plan to use to attach two of the carnival rollercoaster carts together?

13 What does Count Olaf in the disguise of Mattathias order on his first day at the hospital?

14 Which member of the Snow Scouts does the boy in the sweater say is a light sleeper?

15 In *The Bad Beginning*, what did Count Olaf put Sunny inside to leave her dangling outside his tower?

16 In *The Ersatz Elevator*, who took the children around the city after Esmé Squalor left for work?

17 People who lived in the lumbermill dormitory were only allowed visitors on a Sunday: true or false?

18 In *The Ersatz Elevator*, what did the man in sunglasses say the letters V.F.D. stood for?

19 According to Klaus, what needed to be completed before the hospital operation on Violet could be performed?

20 Which visitor to Dr Montgomery's house turned out to have hooks for hands?

21 What drink did Violet and Klaus both order at the Anxious Clown restaurant?

22 What was the name of the doctor who had donated the book *Advanced Ocular Science* to the lumbermill library?

23 There was a list of books in Vice Principal Nero's letter to Mr and Mrs Spats. What was the name of the Roald Dahl book on this list: *Matilda, The Minpins* or *The Twits*?

24 Which one of the following was not a chapter in the book, *Advanced Ocular Science*: Itchy Eyelashes, Sunglasses, Squinting For Profit or Winking Problems?

25 In V.F.D. village, who had the only key to the uptown jail?

26 Sir's arrival caused someone to step backwards into the line of the lumbermill saw blade. Who was this?

27 In *The Ersatz Elevator*, whose voice could the children hear above them as they trekked down the secret passageway?

28　In *The Slippery Slope*, two letters were written in the top of the boysenberry jam – the the letter 'j' and what other letter?

29　What was the name of the lighthouse just to the west of Curdled Cove?

30　When Count Olaf met Violet, Klaus and Sunny for the very first time, what item of clothing was he not wearing: trousers, shoes, socks or a shirt?

31　What age must Violet be to inherit the Baudelaire fortune?

32　What sort of food is Hector's specialty: Chinese, Mexican or Italian?

33　Who is the Vice President of Orphan Affairs at Mulctuary Money Management: Arthur Poe, Edward Smithjones or Roberto Spats?

34　In which building on Prufrock School's grounds were the exams overseen by the Vice Principal to take place?

35　Which one of the following was not part of Dr Montgomery's reptile collection: a two-headed lizard, a toad with wings, a frog with three eyes or a snake with three mouths?

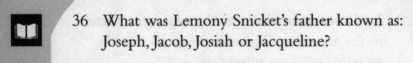

36 What was Lemony Snicket's father known as: Joseph, Jacob, Josiah or Jacqueline?

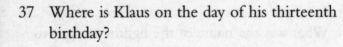

37 Where is Klaus on the day of his thirteenth birthday?

38 Who says that Duncan Quagmire is Violet's boyfriend?

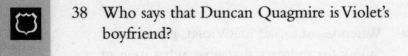

39 In *The Reptile Room*, what time does the *Prospero* leave its dock to sail: three o'clock, five o'clock, seven o'clock or nine o'clock?

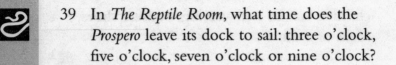

40 When Madame Lulu suggests Count Olaf takes a shower, Olaf says he last showered how many days ago?

41 What was the colour of the wig Shirley was wearing: black, ginger, blonde or brown?

42 Which two characters burned down the Caligari Carnival fortune-telling tent?

43 What sort of trees grew in the lands ruled by Queen Debbie in Lemony Snicket's story?

44 In Snicket's unauthorized autobiography, what was the name of the ship that left from Daedalus Dock over three hours early?

45   What present did Aunt Josephine buy Sunny?

46   In *The Bad Beginning*, which actor was holding a walkie-talkie throughout the entire play, according to the bald man?

47   Which one of the Quagmire children writes poetry?

48   Which child investigated the library in the burned down V.F.D. headquarters for any surviving documents?

49   What is the name of the woman who is Head of Human Resources at Heimlich Hospital?

50   Which of the five children climbed up the ladder to Hector's flying machine first?

QUIZ 17

1   Did Count Olaf and the man with hooks for hands escape in: Mr Poe's car, Uncle Monty's jeep or Dr Lucafont's car?

2   Was Mr Poe looking for the Quagmire children in: the mountains, on the sea or in a desert?

MISERABLY MEDIUM QUESTIONS

3 Captain Sham, Mr Poe and the Baudelaire children ate the Extra Fun Special Family Appetizer for their lunch: true or false?

4 Which adult panicked when he saw Sunny bitten by the Incredibly Deadly Viper?

5 Close to the Swarthy Swamp there lies a factory making: steel poles, horseradish or deck chairs?

6 What was Dr Orwell's first name?

7 What birthday present did Tony want from Queen Debbie: a myna bird, a cake or diamonds?

8 In Isadora's poem, what would she rather do than spend time with Carmelita Spats?

9 In *The Bad Beginning*, who stayed up all night reading a law book to uncover Count Olaf's evil plan?

10 Jonah Mapple lay in Room 201 in Heimlich Hospital, but was he suffering from: toothache, seasickness or the plague?

11 In what act of the play *The Marvelous Marriage* were Klaus and Violet to appear on stage?

MISERABLY MEDIUM QUESTIONS

12 What type of snake was in the cage covered in a cloth: the Mamba du Mal, the Incredibly Deadly Viper or the Hungarian Sloth Snake?

13 What was the name of the toy doll Aunt Josephine bought Violet?

14 In *The Vile Village*, who revealed they were carrying a harpoon gun hidden underneath a blanket?

15 A burned note leads Violet, Klaus and Quigley to what item in the ruined V.F.D. headquarters?

16 What pasta sauce was Captain Sham eating when he was attacked by leeches: carbonara, puttanesca or cheese 'n' garlic?

17 Which brothers' fairy tales were on the list of books in Vice Principal Nero's letter to Mr and Mrs Spats?

18 Where do Hector and the children have their first meal in V.F.D. village: in the barn, in Hector's house, outside on the porch or in the Nevermore Tree?

19 Which one of the carnival freaks cooked a Thai soup in the caravan?

MISERABLY MEDIUM QUESTIONS

20 What was the name of the museum in the city that Violet was relieved still contained her favourite exhibits?

21 At a masked ball, what did Baron van de Wetering come dressed as: an oak tree, a jar of marmalade or a 4 metre high cat?

22 As Sunny slept in the casserole dish on the mountainside, what did she use as a blanket?

23 Who was to be Klaus' teacher at Prufrock School: Mr Nero, Mr Remora or Mrs Bass?

24 In *The Wide Window*, who grabbed Aunt Josephine's hairnet off her head?

25 As Madame Lulu led the Baudelaire children through the carnival, what did she hold in her hand?

26 At the In Auction, who slipped on the doilies and fell to the ground: Jerome, Violet, Gunther or Klaus?

27 Violet dropped something next to the door to Dr Montgomery's kitchen, so she would have an excuse if anyone spotted her listening in on the adults' conversation. What was it?

MISERABLY MEDIUM QUESTIONS

28 According to Klaus, an Egyptian king did impressions when he was hypnotised. Were they: seal impressions, chicken impressions or dog impressions?

29 Why did Coach Ghengis say he could not take his training shoes off?

30 In the Heimlich Hospital, was the Head of Human Resources' office the seventh, ninth, seventeenth or nineteenth door on the left?

31 What was the name of the boat the Baudelaires and Uncle Monty were to sail on to Peru?

32 Whose house slid down the hill and into Lake Lachrymose?

33 In *The Hostile Hospital*, what was Violet's jumbled up name on the patient list: Ed Valiantbrue, Laura V. Bleediotie or Albert E. Deviloeia?

34 Where does Count Olaf want to hide the Quagmire children until he can get hold of their fortune: in a mountain range, on an island, in an oasis in the desert or at the North Pole?

MISERABLY MEDIUM QUESTIONS

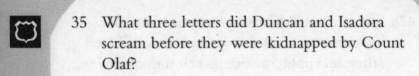

35 What three letters did Duncan and Isadora scream before they were kidnapped by Count Olaf?

36 Beginning with the letter 'd', what was the name of the famous detective assigned to solve Jacques' murder?

37 Just after Klaus, Violet and Sunny met their new guardian in *The Miserable Mill*, who gave them a peach to share for lunch?

38 What item does Lemony Snicket say he stole from Esmé Squalor's apartment?

39 What was the name of the man who greeted the children at the Prufrock School dormitory?

40 Is Count Olaf's tattoo of a dragon, an eye, a lion or a sword?

41 Esmé's new dress looked like flames and crackled as she walked: true or false?

42 What caused a shadow over the whole of V.F.D. at sunset time?

43 As Klaus and Violet began their journey to find Sunny, who carried the pitcher?

MISERABLY MEDIUM QUESTIONS

44 Lemony Snicket explains how in one job interview he had to hit what with a bow and arrow: an apple, an olive, a lemon or an ant?

45 What item in the V.F.D. village jail cell does Violet say they can use as a sponge?

46 What was the name of the restaurant in Lake Lachrymose that Lemony Snicket is advised to visit by his brother?

47 Who entered the operating theatre with the real Dr Tocuna and Nurse Flo?

48 In *The Ersatz Elevator*, what did the children use to bang on the ceiling of the secret passageway?

49 Who was guarding the room where Foreman Flacutono and Shirley were held?

50 What item did Count Olaf's gang use to connect his car to the carnival caravan?

QUIZ 18

1 Who escaped from the In Auction along with Count Olaf?

MISERABLY MEDIUM QUESTIONS

2   What was the name of the newspaper which contained a story about a man strangling a bishop: *The Hong Kong Times, The Bangkok Gazette* or *The Singapore Bugle*?

3   What part did the book *Advanced Ocular Science* play in Count Olaf's escape from the lumbermill?

4   Who flattered Aunt Josephine about her age and invited her out for a cup of tea the next time she was in town?

5   In *The Slippery Slope*, which one of Count Olaf's gang had a dream about sneezing and giving people germs?

6   The V.F.D. disguise kit contains a blazer of what colour?

7   What was contained in the caged trailer Count Olaf's car pulled to the Caligari Carnival?

8   In *The Slippery Slope*, who climbs the frozen waterfall along with Violet?

9   What does Duncan Quagmire want to be when he's older?

MISERABLY MEDIUM QUESTIONS

10 Of the adults the Baudelaire children met in
The Reptile Room, what was the name of
the man who smoked a cigar?

11 What item did Count Olaf flourish as the
Caligari Carnival show began?

12 What colour is the cover of Lemony Snicket's
notebook: green, blue or red?

13 At the start of *The Wide Window*, where did
Violet, Klaus and Sunny head to after their
aunt's house was destroyed?

14 What colour was Count Olaf's blazer?

15 Who entered the operating theatre to say that
the Heimlich Hospital's Library of Records
was on fire?

16 Which of the Baudelaire children were
tripped up by Foreman Flacutono?

17 When the two-headed freak is interviewed by
Madame Lulu, what name does Violet give to
her half?

18 Who ripped up Stephano's ticket for the ship
crossing to Peru?

19 Who bought Klaus a book of Finnish poetry for his eighth birthday?

20 Which one of the following was not a chore for the children on their first working day in V.F.D.: wash Mr Lesko's windows, fold up all the chairs in the Town Hall, cut Mrs Morrow's hedges?

21 For which meal did Captain Sham meet the children at the Anxious Clown: breakfast, lunch or dinner?

22 Who brought Vice Principal Nero a rose to congratulate him on his violin concert?

23 At which hospital was Sunny Baudelaire born: Pincus, St Peter's or Woebetide Hospital?

24 What sort of clothing did Sunny and Klaus put on from the supply cupboard at Heimlich Hospital?

25 In *The Ersatz Elevator*, how did the children get out of the secret passageway: unlocking a small door, climbing up a wooden ladder, opening a trap door or swimming through a lake?

MISERABLY MEDIUM QUESTIONS

26 Can you name two of the three volunteers who reported to Babs' office to work at the Heimlich Hospital's Library of Records?

27 In *The Slippery Slope*, who used a toboggan to travel down the mountain slope to the source of the green smoke: Sunny, Count Olaf or Esmé?

28 The first shot from the harpoon gun destroyed Hector's supply of what fruit juice: cranberry, orange, apple or grapefruit?

29 In *The Austere Academy*, in which room were Klaus' lessons held?

30 Who explains to Mr Poe that the Incredibly Deadly Viper is not dangerous: Dr Lucafont, Violet Baudelaire, Stephano or Klaus?

31 Who had to ride in the carnival caravan towed by Count Olaf's car: Kevin and Hugo, Esmé and Sunny or Klaus and Violet?

32 What colour were the eyes of the Incredibly Deadly Viper snake?

33 How many windows were found in the Lucky Smells Lumbermill dormitory building: one, three, five or none?

34 What does Aunt Josephine use to stop burglars in the rooms of her house?

35 What is the first name of Mr Poe's wife: Patty, Polly or Pandora?

36 How long does Sunny say it takes her to open one of the hospital's locked filing cabinets: 10 minutes, an hour, several hours or an entire day?

37 Where were Sunny and Violet when they heard the lumbermill saw machine turned on in the middle of the night?

38 Which Baudelaire child ties her hair up with ribbons when she's thinking?

39 In *The Carnivorous Carnival*, whose motto is 'give people what they want'?

40 Since the schism, members of the V.F.D. no longer have to get what item of body decoration?

41 As Violet travelled through the Mortmain Mountains, what did she wear over her clothes to try and keep warm: a fur coat, a poncho, an ugly striped sweater or a blazer?

MISERABLY MEDIUM QUESTIONS

42 What food does Hector cook for Klaus, Sunny and Violet's first meal in V.F.D.: chicken enchiladas, beef tortillas or chilli and rice?

43 In the Baudelaire children's room at Count Olaf's house, how many beds were there for the three of them?

44 Can you name either of the children Count Olaf plans to hide inside one of the auction items?

45 When Violet rubbed the oar along the side of the boat on Lake Lachrymose, was she trying to: make a certain sound, start a fire, or scrape off the leeches?

46 In *The Unauthorized Autobiography*, the meeting notes of the Building Committee show that they are to meet at 7.30pm to see what film?

47 In Stephano's room, a half dozen of what sort of bottle stood on the dresser?

48 In *The Austere Academy*, which two children were dragged into Count Olaf's getaway car?

49 In *The Ersatz Elevator*, what did the children use to make a trail of crumbs through the penthouse?

50   What item of woman's clothing was Count Olaf wearing which was printed with the eye symbol?

QUIZ 19

1   The second shot from the harpoon gun hit Hector's supply of: wheat flour and batteries, cranberry juice, apples and oranges or firewood and eggs?

2   In *The Hostile Hospital*, whose hand does Sunny bite to help in the children's escape from the operating theatre?

3   Who was the first to say the words 'I do' during *The Marvelous Marriage* play starring Count Olaf?

4   When Madame Lulu interviews the two-headed freak for a place at the carnival, what name does Klaus give to his half?

5   In *The Ersatz Elevator*, who does the man with hooks for hands turn out to be: the man with sunglasses, Jerome Squalor, the doorman or Gunther?

MISERABLY MEDIUM QUESTIONS

6   What is Dr Montgomery's first name?

7   Which one of Count Olaf's gang visited the freaks in their caravan?

8   Esmé Squalor's In Auction is held at what hall?

9   According to Babs, what is the most important thing done at Heimlich Hospital?

10 Amongst Count Olaf's theatre troupe were two women whose faces were covered in what coloured powder?

11 In *The Austere Academy*, who managed to pull off Coach Ghengis' turban?

12 In *The Slippery Slope*, as Violet climbed the frozen waterfall, what item did she use to test the ice ahead of her?

13 On the expedition to Peru, what snake did Uncle Monty plan to carry for safe-keeping?

14 In Lemony Snicket's message to his editor, where does he say the manuscript of *The Austere Academy* is hidden: in a theatre seat, inside some dry cleaning or inside a tree?

MISERABLY MEDIUM QUESTIONS

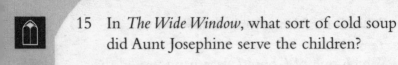

15 In *The Wide Window*, what sort of cold soup did Aunt Josephine serve the children?

16 In Stephano's room at Dr Montgomery's house, what had Stephano blown his nose on repeatedly?

17 Which Prufrock School girl became Coach Ghengis' special messenger?

18 In *The Slippery Slope*, what sort of trap did Klaus, Violet and Quigley build in order to capture Esmé Squalor?

19 In *The Austere Academy*, what does Vice Principal Nero say happens to schoolchildren who are late for class?

20 In *The Hostile Hospital*, when the Baudelaire children switched Hal's keys for pretend ones, what did they use to make the loop for the keys to hang on?

21 What meal did Aunt Josephine prepare for the Baudelaire children the evening after they had met Captain Sham for the first time?

22 What are the walls of the Deluxe Cell in V.F.D. village made of: straw and mud, bricks and mortar, wooden slats or metal plates?

23 Who did the Incredibly Deadly Viper bite on the chin?

24 Which group did Klaus and Sunny join in order to walk round the Heimlich Hospital without being noticed?

25 Who pushed Aunt Josephine overboard to her death in Lachrymose Lake?

26 What did the crabs in the shack not like: red, loud noises, garlic or the violin?

27 Where did Klaus and Violet head in order to avoid the snow gnats?

28 In *The Vile Village*, what large item was Count Olaf using to cover much of his face: a mask, sunglasses or a floppy hat?

29 Who rescued the Baudelaire children and Aunt Josephine in his boat?

30 According to Lemony Snicket's unauthorized autobiography, the jewelled cane in the V.F.D. disguise kit turns into what weapon?

31 Which of the Baudelaire children took a law book from Justice Strauss' library and hid it underneath their shirt?

MISERABLY MEDIUM QUESTIONS

32 At Prufrock School, who is supposed to be making staples all night: Isadora, Sunny, Carmelita or Mrs Bass?

33 Charles took Klaus to an eye doctor in Paltryville. What was the doctor's name?

34 On the children's first day at work in V.F.D. village, what sort of sandwiches were they given for lunch?

35 In *The Hostile Hospital*, what did Sunny and Klaus use to cover much of their faces when they disguised themselves?

36 There is a drawing of Lemony Snicket's family tree in *The Unauthorized Autobiography*. What grim item is dangling from a branch?

37 What button on the walkie-talkie did the children have to press to speak to Count Olaf?

38 Captain Sham's sailboat rental business was housed in what sort of building: a mansion, a block of flats, a large covered dock or a shack?

39 What sort of breakfast did Count Olaf leave for the Baudelaire children every morning at his home: stale bread, lumpy oatmeal, cold fried eggs or rotten apples?

MISERABLY MEDIUM QUESTIONS

40 Who did Violet and Sunny see was tied to a
log at the Lucky Smells Lumbermill in the
middle of the night?

41 Which of Uncle Monty's snakes cried when
the Baudelaire children waved goodbye?

42 Which is the correct word to describe a
group of crows: a flock, a shriek, a murder or
a torture?

43 What was the name of the burger meal at the
Anxious Clown with the sauce and pickles
making a smiley face?

44 Sunny mentioned a fairy tale to suggest how
the children could stop getting lost in the
Squalors' penthouse. Which fairy tale was this?

45 What was the name of the foreman of the
Lucky Smells Lumbermill who left a week
before the Baudelaire children arrived?

46 Which member of Count Olaf's gang is
mistaken as a freak in the carnival?

47 When the children got out of the secret
passageway, what sort of worker did they see
first: a milkman, a postman, a policeman or a
doctor?

48 Which man had grown his fingernails long and painted them with pink nail varnish as part of his disguise as a woman?

49 Which one of the following was not a headquarters for the V.F.D.: 1485 Columbia Road, the Statue of Liberty or the Versailles Post Office?

50 How does Violet say she plans to get the Quagmire children out of the cage: by picking the lock, by sawing through the bars or by welding?

TRAGICALLY TOUGH QUESTIONS

QUIZ 1

1 What was the name of the fountain found in the banking district of the city the Baudelaire children lived in?

2 What was Aunt Josephine's surname?

3 Lemony Snicket's column in *The Daily Punctilio* was replaced by Geraldine Julienne's – but what was her column called?

4 In *The Miserable Mill*, what was the word that unhypnotised Klaus?

5 As Count Olaf entered the fortune-telling tent with Esmé and surprised Sunny, Klaus and Violet, what was he holding?

6 What was the name of the river which the children had visited with their parents and eaten sticky shrimp and picked blackberries?

7 What was the name of the man who was director of marketing for the Herpetological Society?

8 In the *Zombies in the Snow* film mentioned in Lemony Snicket's unauthorized autobiography, what is the name of the character who builds a snowman?

9 In *The Hostile Hospital*, what device does Violet fashion out of an empty alphabet soup tin?

10 Can you name either of Mr Poe's sons?

11 What did Foreman Flacutono bang together to wake up the lumbermill workers?

12 What was the first meal the Baudelaire children had to eat at Prufrock School with just their hands?

13 In *The Unauthorized Autobiography*, Meredith Heuer supplied a blurry photo of what building?

14 What did Uncle Monty's roommate do when he was a student to his prized toad specimen?

15 In *The Slippery Slope*, Sunny overheard Count Olaf say the name of the volunteers' last safe place. What was it?

16 What was the first name of Aunt Josephine's husband?

17 In Count Olaf's house, the Baudelaire's room was furnished with only a box, a bed, and a pile of what?

18 In *The Slippery Slope*, what was the name of the cave's chimney which also acted as a secret passageway and had a name which could be shortened to V.F.D.?

19 Which two of the following things were in objects according to the King of Arizona: nectarines, magenta wallpaper, billboards with weasels on them, purple cereal bowls?

20 What sentence is written along the bottom of the second ticket to the Prospero ship, displayed in Lemony Snicket's unauthorized autobiography?

21 What was the name of the patient at Heimlich Hospital who had terrible toothache?

22 In *The Bad Beginning*, the man who organised the lighting at the theatre had what all over his face?

23 How many folds were there in the piece of paper containing the name of the carnival freak to be thrown to the lions?

24 What did Sunny do after she was bitten on the chin by the Incredibly Deadly Viper?

25 What was the name of the book featuring the Lucky Smells Lumbermill owner on the cover?

26 According to the V.F.D. disguise notes, what one item do you need to disguise yourself as a taxi driver?

27 What was the name of the mountain Jerome said he had hiked up with Klaus, Violet and Sunny's mother around 20 years ago?

28 Which village did Mr Poe not want the children to live in because he did not like the bank there?

29 In *The Carnivorous Carnival*, what is the name of the queen's boyfriend in Lemony Snicket's short fairy story?

30 After Sunny had been brought to the theatre, what food did she cry for?

31 In *The Wide Window*, what was the name of the clothing store the children saw close to the docks?

32 In *The Hostile Hospital*, what does Count Olaf promise that the henchman or woman who captures the Baudelaire children can do that same evening?

33 What was the name of the mechanical instructor at the V.F.D. headquarters who Lemony Snicket writes about?

34 In *The Miserable Mill*, what was the name of the only prize Lemony Snicket reckons the Baudelaire children would win?

35 In Lemony Snicket's unauthorized autobiography, Esmé, the actress, writes a letter to which newspaper reporter?

36 What does Lemony Snicket say he was disguised as at the Duchess of Winnipeg's ball?

37 As the children climbed to meet their new guardians in the penthouse apartment, on what floor did they hear the sound of someone taking a bath?

38 In *The Carnivorous Carnival*, what item belonging to the newspaper reporter did the man with hooks for hands get his hook caught in?

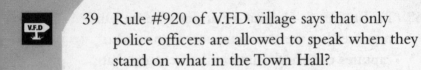

39 Rule #920 of V.F.D. village says that only police officers are allowed to speak when they stand on what in the Town Hall?

40 Which creature in Uncle Monty's collection did he warn not to let anywhere near a typewriter?

41 In the photograph found in *The Hostile Hospital*, what was the figure turned away from the camera holding in his hands?

42 After Dr Montgomery's house was burned down, to which town or village did Quigley head?

43 At the In Auction, how much was Sunny's final bid for Lot #50?

44 How long was the intermission between two parts of the play, *The Marvelous Marriage*?

45 In *The Carnivorous Carnival*, who says to the Baudelaire children that they used to be a noble person and wonder if they could be noble again?

46 What was the name of the nurse who accompanied Dr Tocuna?

47 In *The Unauthorized Autobiography*, what was the name of the wedding arrangers which sent a coded message to Lemony Snicket warning him not to visit them?

48 What was placed jutting over the top of the lion's pit?

49 In *The Ersatz Elevator*, what was the name of the hall which regularly won the Door Prize in the city?

50 When the fire that destroyed Quigley's home was started, in which room was he sitting?

EXCRUCIATINGLY EASY ANSWERS

QUIZ 1

1. Baudelaire
2. *The Hostile Hospital*
3. Count Olaf
4. Violet
5. Count Olaf
6. Sunny Baudelaire
7. Three
8. Snakes
9. Crows
10. Green

11. Chewing gum
12. Aunt Josephine
13. Hugo
14. Klaus
15. The violin
16. Hector
17. Uncle Monty
18. Paltryville
19. Esmé Squalor
20. Hal

21. Coach Ghengis
22. Violet
23. Salmon
24. Aunt Josephine
25. Sunny

26. Theatre critic
27. Madame Lulu
28. Burning at the stake
29. Two
30. Captain Sham

31. V.F.D.
32. False
33. Lake Lachrymose
34. Four
35. Coach Ghengis
36. True
37. Count Olaf
38. Sunny
39. Rubber bands
40. Snakes

41. The left
42. Esmé Squalor
43. A tattoo
44. A shack
45. Forks
46. Milk
47. Count Olaf
48. She hired them
49. Klaus' glasses
50. On his ankle

MISERABLY MEDIUM ANSWERS

QUIZ 1

1. Lake Lachrymose
2. 500 degrees
3. Beef casserole
4. A lamp
5. Dr Montgomery
6. Mr Poe
7. 66
8. The Village of Fowl Devotees
9. Jerome and Esmé Squalor
10. Aunt Josephine

11. Count Olaf (Officer Dupin)
12. Esmé Squalor
13. Lousy Lane
14. A brass reading lamp
15. 11
16. The Administrative Building
17. True
18. A piece of sail
19. The Finite Forest
20. Esmé Squalor

21. Her left hand
22. *The Daily Punctilio*
23. Four
24. Corn on the cob
25. Hair ribbon

26. Klaus
27. *The Daily Punctilio*
28. *The Bad Beginning*
29. The person who could be a man or a woman
30. A French admiral

31. The 's' aisle
32. Pink
33. Isadora
34. In a caravan
35. The lions
36. An eye
37. Quigley
38. 19
39. Dark Avenue
40. A poem

41. *The Reptile Room*
42. Klaus
43. Five years of age
44. The Last Chance General Store
45. Justice Strauss
46. Esmé Squalor's lap
47. Metal
48. The letter 'b'
49. From bullet holes
50. A mask

QUIZ 2

1. *Zombies in the Snow*
2. Snicket
3. Kevin
4. A Count
5. Colette
6. Four
7. Hot fudge sundaes
8. Blue
9. Paltryville
10. Count Olaf

11. The toboggan
12. Special Orphan Running Exercises
13. True
14. Julio
15. Chewing gum
16. Esmé Squalor
17. Gustav
18. On the stairs
19. The rope ladder
20. One

21. A tuba
22. Rarely Ridden Road
23. In Count Olaf's tower
24. Iced coffee

25. A door knob
26. Mr Remora
27. Grim River
28. Glasses
29. Stamping
30. Cinnamon

31. Mount Fraught
32. Omar
33. A sugar bowl
34. The movies
35. True
36. Foreman Flacutono
37. A bicycle wheel
38. Sawdust
39. Six hours
40. Over 300 years

41. Sunny Baudelaire
42. White wine
43. Esmé Squalor
44. Electrical devices
45. Damocles Dock
46. Prufrock Preparatory School
47. False teeth
48. Black
49. Third
50. Whistle

QUIZ 3

1. Klaus
2. Lucky
3. Miss Tench
4. Mr Poe
5. Red
6. The 'j' aisle
7. Violet
8. Three
9. True
10. Beatrice

11. Fire tongs
12. Brett Helquist
13. The sugar bowl
14. True
15. Foreman Flacutono
16. Salmon
17. A linen napkin
18. Torch it (burn it down)
19. Lou
20. The ruins of their parents' home

21. Dominoes
22. The Not-Very-Supermarket
23. A circle
24. Mountbank

25. 30 feet
26. Mr Poe
27. Three
28. Three
29. Violet Baudelaire
30. The Herpetological Society

31. Carmelita Spats
32. The Fowl Fountain
33. Stephano
34. Basement
35. Caligari Carnival
36. A bag of flour
37. *The Austere Academy*
38. Gunther
39. Sunny
40. Captain Sham

41. The Reptile Room
42. Mr Poe
43. 667 Dark Avenue
44. Coupons
45. Green peppers
46. *Zombies in the Snow*
47. Peppermints
48. Three
49. Violet
50. A hair ribbon

QUIZ 4

1. A monocle
2. *The Vile Village*
3. The school kitchen
4. Hammocks
5. Count Olaf
6. Bus
7. The fortune-telling tent
8. Café Salmonella
9. False
10. Mr Poe

11. Vice Principal Nero
12. Mr Poe
13. Lemony and Beatrice
14. Two
15. Captain Sham
16. False
17. Miss Bass
18. Tape
19. Café Salmonella
20. Fowl Fountain

21. *The World Is Quiet Here*
22. Their notebooks
23. Once
24. The Deluxe Cell
25. An actor

26. The Fowl Fountain
27. False
28. Aunt Josephine
29. Stone
30. St Carl's Cathedral

31. In the library
32. Baudelaire
33. Violet Baudelaire
34. Bring Count Olaf's troupe some potato chips
35. Eagles
36. Carmelita Spats
37. Helicopter
38. Count Olaf
39. Fourteen
40. Klaus

41. Beverley and Elliot
42. Soap
43. Klaus
44. Babs
45. A glass window
46. Two
47. Three
48. Friendly
49. Nothing
50. White-hot

QUIZ 5

1. *Wombats on Ice*
2. Oval-shaped
3. The hinterlands
4. Square
5. Sunny
6. Violet
7. Gunther
8. Klaus
9. Creamed spinach, a fork, a potato
10. Violet

11. The library
12. Hazy Harbour
13. Kevin
14. Peppermints
15. Esmé Squalor
16. *The Slippery Slope*
17. Officer Luciana
18. Squalor
19. Lucky Smells Lumbermill
20. A detective badge on a gold chain

21. The V.F.D. headquarters
22. The wooden bench
23. Grey
24. A net

25. A casserole dish
26. The Town Hall
27. Poured it onto the caravan's wheels
28. Violet's
29. A safari suit
30. Half-finished

31. Aunt Josephine's atlas
32. Star-shaped
33. A harpoon
34. Volunteers Fighting Disease
35. One
36. Dr Orwell
37. Schools
38. Sloppy eating
39. Isadora and Duncan
40. One

41. The King of Arizona
42. Dr Orwell
43. White
44. Oven mitts
45. True
46. Sunny's
47. Right-handed
48. Stamping
49. Randall
50. Pinstripe suits

QUIZ 6

1. A business card
2. A rollercoaster
3. Three
4. Coach Ghengis
5. Sunny
6. An auction catalogue
7. Lemonade
8. Briny Beach
9. Jacques
10. His tongue swells up

11. *Lawyers in the Jungle*
12. Bales of hay
13. A crab's claw
14. Dr Lucafont
15. 45 minutes
16. Her parents
17. An eggplant (aubergine)
18. Snake poison
19. Carmelita Spats
20. Carrots

21. A long knife
22. Charles
23. Five
24. K
25. The two women with white powder on their faces

26. He is hypnotised
27. Sunny
28. Two
29. Four
30. Klaus, Violet

31. Justice Strauss
32. In a barn
33. The Sumac
34. The second floor
35. In the fortune-telling tent
36. Five
37. Too large
38. An old shoe
39. Count Olaf
40. A policeman's helmet

41. Three
42. Dr Montgomery
43. *The Austere Academy*
44. Raspberries
45. A vase
46. Phil
47. Ben
48. Coconut cream cake
49. The ante-chamber
50. Six

QUIZ 7

1. Klaus
2. Seven
3. A monocle
4. The Veritable French Diner
5. The Wide Window
6. Madame Lulu
7. Ballet shoes made of chocolate
8. Unbearable
9. Snow Scouts
10. The Devil's Tongue

11. 922
12. False
13. A starfish
14. Esmé Squalor
15. True
16. Dirt under his fingernails
17. Veronica
18. Sunny
19. *The Marvelous Marriage*
20. She breaks out into a rash (hives)

21. Violet Baudelaire
22. The Barbary Chewer
23. Hot dog vendor
24. Cranberry muffins

25. A potato
26. Sunny
27. On the arch in front of the school
28. White marble
29. A treasure map
30. Windows

31. A padlock
32. Madame Lulu
33. The Inky Newt
34. A debarker
35. Its eye
36. A safe
37. Crabs
38. Klaus
39. 612 clocks
40. The Snicket file

41. Crows
42. The string machine
43. Light and elevators
44. Sunny
45. Sapphires
46. An automatic rolling pin
47. Hector
48. An eye
49. Mr Poe
50. True

QUIZ 8

1. Klaus
2. One
3. Mr Poe
4. Violet Baudelaire
5. Uncle Monty's
6. Chewing gum
7. Duncan and Isadora Quagmire
8. A crow
9. The up button
10. Aunt Josephine

11. Canned peaches
12. True
13. A carrot
14. Madame Lulu
15. The table
16. First
17. Milt
18. Rule #201
19. The Lachrymose Leeches
20. Two

21. Esmé Squalor
22. Wednesday
23. Mr Poe
24. Foreman Flacutono, Shirley (Count Olaf)
25. Nine

26. Violet
27. Gunther
28. Esmé Squalor
29. True
30. A bread knife

31. Accommodating
32. False
33. Duncan and Isadora Quagmire
34. Seagulls
35. Foreman Flacutono
36. The ninth floor
37. 12
38. A peppermint
39. Kevin
40. Finnish women in the fifteenth century

41. False
42. She got sunburned
43. Sir
44. Green
45. Madame Lulu's crystal ball
46. Count Olaf's car
47. Creamed spinach
48. *The Daily Punctilio*
49. Her shoulder
50. Place them in a bowl

QUIZ 9

1. Uptown
2. A widow
3. An enormous globe
4. The sound of the water
5. Al Funcoot
6. False
7. The bald man
8. Mr Poe's house
9. Shirley
10. Eye-shaped

11. Stephano
12. Slide down the banisters
13. Coins
14. The man with hooks for hands
15. Burn them
16. Quigley Quagmire
17. Blue
18. A fork
19. Dr Orwell
20. The Mamba du Mal

21. A sock
22. Venom du Mal
23. Telephone
24. False
25. Both things happen

26. The Crystal Ballroom
27. A motorcycle helmet
28. The doorman
29. Stricken Stream
30. A sugar bowl

31. Madame Lulu
32. Six
33. True
34. Cups and bowls
35. Esmé Squalor (Officer Luciana)
36. Rancorous Rocks, Wicked Whirlpool
37. Wholesome
38. Coach Ghengis
39. Five
40. Mr Poe's

41. The children's mother
42. On a farm
43. A beard
44. Klaus
45. Hector
46. Madame Lulu
47. Latin
48. A ski pole
49. Violet
50. Grey

QUIZ 10

1. Isadora
2. Beatrice
3. The Fowl Fountain
4. Eyebrows
5. A pig contest
6. Dr Montgomery's (Uncle Monty's)
7. A tube sock
8. Café Kafka
9. Hurricane Herman
10. In his barn

11. Remember, you will die
12. The Fish District
13. Peru
14. Phil
15. A shiny whistle
16. Quigley Quagmire
17. False spring rolls
18. Madame Lulu
19. Esmé Squalor
20. An aqueous martini

21. Ukulele
22. The Council of Elders
23. Madame Lulu
24. In a fire
25. Three

26. A hair ribbon
27. A sword
28. Esmé Squalor
29. That the cave was for sale
30. Count Olaf's house

31. Three
32. Snakes' venom
33. Klaus
34. An eye
35. Taxi
36. V.F.D.
37. True
38. The man with hooks for hands
39. A guitar
40. Olivia

41. The files about the Snicket fires
42. A peach
43. Neckties
44. False
45. Chocolate
46. Xylophone
47. Stephano
48. V.F.D.
49. Sally
50. Carmelita Spats

QUIZ 11

1. Lasagne
2. Red
3. *Handbook for Advanced Apostrophe Use*
4. Esmé Squalor
5. Pasta
6. Carrier pigeons
7. Salmon
8. Snails
9. The Esmé Squalor Fan Club
10. Jerome Squalor

11. Count Olaf
12. Jacques Snicket
13. A campground
14. From the boot of Count Olaf's car
15. The children's luggage
16. The Nevermore Tree
17. Sunny
18. A piece of rope
19. True
20. Klaus, Sunny and Violet

21. A footstool
22. His mother
23. His eighth banana
24. A stream

25. Dr Orwell
26. White
27. Hooks for hands
28. A tip
29. Dark Avenue
30. White

31. Saturday
32. The Boss
33. Mr Poe
34. A powder puff
35. A shopping list
36. Dr Montgomery's house
37. No news is good news
38. *The Prospero*
39. Cigar smoke
40. A left wooden leg

41. Esmé Squalor
42. Horseradish
43. The Devil's Tongue
44. The fortune-telling tent
45. Sunny
46. One hour
47. Cheer and applaud
48. Sunny
49. A walkie-talkie
50. Hats in the shape of crows

QUIZ 12

1. Salmon fritters
2. Charles
3. Count Olaf
4. Mr Poe
5. A lens from a pair of glasses
6. Two
7. Justice Strauss
8. Jacques Snicket
9. Mrs Poe
10. An old man

11. Officer Luciana
12. Two
13. A bag of sweets
14. Daniel Handler
15. Esmé Squalor
16. Al Funcoot
17. The Veritable French Diner
18. Mrs Morrow
19. Four
20. They were ill-fitting

21. Klaus
22. Boiled cabbage
23. Valley of Four Drafts
24. Hal
25. Mortmain Mountains

26. Pink
27. The rest of the day
28. The Reptile Room
29. Green
30. Klaus Baudelaire

31. A canoe
32. Brr!
33. Freaks
34. The big red fish statue
35. Hugo
36. Mr Remora
37. A door knob
38. A big dress
39. Lake Lachrymose
40. A sweatshirt

41. Under her bed
42. Klaus
43. Klaus
44. The storage shed
45. Sapphires
46. Dr Orwell
47. Cheerful
48. A beard
49. Geniveve, Gigi
50. A supply cupboard

QUIZ 13

1. A large library
2. Ocean decorating
3. Her teeth
4. Dr Flacutono
5. A waterfall
6. A box of thumbtacks
7. Snow gnats
8. Isadora Quagmire
9. A handkerchief
10. Over three hours

11. Sunny Baudelaire
12. Dr Lucafont
13. Knives
14. The school computer
15. Crows
16. Mrs Bass
17. A stove
18. Sally
19. Count Olaf
20. Charles

21. False
22. Masks
23. A rope net
24. Brown
25. A fridge

26. Ivy
27. Enemies are nearby
28. 29
29. Nothing
30. Shirley

31. A long knife
32. A wooden bench
33. Count Olaf
34. Crow feathers
35. Vice Principal Nero
36. Lemony Snicket
37. Esmé Squalor
38. Peppermints
39. White
40. Violet and Klaus

41. Jacques Snicket
42. Schism
43. Phil
44. An eye
45. Duncan Quagmire
46. The radiator
47. Hot chocolate
48. The Anxious Clown
49. Lemony Snicket
50. Mortmain Mountains

QUIZ 14

1. A stuntwoman
2. Vice Principal Nero
3. Violet
4. A sailor's suit
5. Filing cabinets
6. Beige
7. Rule books
8. Mr Remora, Mrs Bass
9. Violet
10. Violet

11. 71
12. A banana
13. Applaud him
14. Debbie
15. Crickets
16. Heart-shaped
17. Yes
18. A lion
19. Larry
20. Dr Lucafont

21. Hector's self-sustaining hot air mobile home
22. Eleanora Poe
23. Mamba du Mal
24. Nevermore Tree

25. Bruce
26. Charles
27. 204
28. Detective Smith
29. Smoke
30. One

31. Klaus
32. Alphabet soup
33. Count Olaf
34. Two
35. Earrings
36. Renting out sailboats
37. Klaus
38. Count Olaf
39. The head
40. Half-person, half-wolf

41. Shirley
42. Sunny Baudelaire
43. A debarker
44. Sugar bowl
45. Chewing gum
46. Green
47. A cage
48. Curdled Cave
49. Three
50. Mr Poe

QUIZ 15

1. Dr Orwell
2. Thursday
3. The knife
4. One
5. Mattathias
6. Parsley soda
7. Be his secretary
8. Valorous Farms Dairy
9. Stroganoff
10. Metal masks

11. A rope ladder
12. Four
13. Captain Sham
14. Jacques
15. Doilies
16. The Heimlich Hospital
17. Coach Ghengis
18. 14 years
19. Mice
20. Clouded Peak

21. Dr Lucafont
22. Hector
23. A ukulele
24. One ear
25. Violet

26. A loaf of bread
27. Religious convictions
28. On her nose
29. Justice Strauss
30. Tall and thin

31. Sunny Baudelaire
32. Dr Sebald
33. A model train set
34. Count Olaf
35. Light brown
36. Lachrymose Leeches
37. Mr Remora
38. None
39. Fire tongs
40. Madame Lulu

41. Klaus
42. 13
43. Isadora
44. Marshmallows
45. Burn it down
46. A filing cabinet
47. Count Olaf
48. Isadora and Duncan Quagmire
49. Midgets
50. Café Salmonella

QUIZ 16

1. Violet
2. Mr Remora
3. Klaus and Aunt Josephine
4. In the school cafeteria
5. Kudzu
6. A glass eye
7. Lachrymose Leeches
8. A workbench
9. Beneath the Nevermore Tree
10. Their notebooks

11. Fire and smoke
12. Ivy
13. An inspection
14. Bruce
15. A birdcage
16. Jerome
17. False
18. Very Fancy Doilies
19. Paperwork
20. Dr Lucafont

21. Water
22. Dr Orwell
23. *Matilda*
24. Squinting for Profit
25. Officer Luciana

26. Dr Orwell
27. The doorman's
28. The letter 's'
29. Lavender Lighthouse
30. Socks

31. 18
32. Mexican food
33. Arthur Poe
34. The shack
35. A frog with three eyes
36. Jacob
37. In jail
38. Vice Principal Nero
39. Five o'clock
40. 10 days ago

41. Blonde
42. Klaus and Violet
43. Lollipop trees
44. *The Prospero*
45. A rattle
46. Count Olaf
47. Isadora
48. Klaus
49. Babs
50. Isadora

QUIZ 17

1. Dr Lucafont's car
2. In the mountains
3. False
4. Mr Poe
5. A horseradish factory
6. Georgina
7. Diamonds
8. Eat a bowl of vampire bats
9. Klaus Baudelaire
10. Seasickness

11. Act Three
12. The Incredibly Deadly Viper
13. Pretty Penny
14. Officer Luciana
15. The fridge
16. Puttanesca
17. The Brothers Grimm
18. Outside on the porch
19. Hugo
20. The Verne Invention Museum

21. An oak tree
22. A dishtowel
23. Mrs Bass
24. Violet
25. A fanbelt
26. Gunther
27. A hair ribbon
28. Chicken impressions
29. His feet were smelly
30. Seventeenth

31. *The Prospero*
32. Aunt Josephine's
33. Laura V. Bleediotie
34. On an island
35. V.F.D.
36. Detective Dupin
37. Charles
38. A sugar bowl
39. Phil
40. An eye

41. True
42. Crows
43. Klaus
44. An olive
45. The loaf of bread
46. The Anxious Clown
47. Esmé Squalor
48. Fire tongs
49. Phil
50. Count Olaf's whip

QUIZ 18

1. Esmé Squalor
2. *The Bangkok Gazette*
3. Count Olaf threw it through the window to escape
4. Captain Sham
5. The man with hooks for hands
6. Turquoise
7. Lions
8. Quigley
9. A newspaper reporter
10. Bruce

11. A whip
12. Green
13. Damocles Dock
14. Turquoise
15. Hal
16. Klaus
17. Beverley
18. Uncle Monty
19. Violet
20. Fold up all the chairs in the Town Hall

21. Lunch
22. Coach Ghengis
23. Pincus Hospital
24. White coats

25. Opening a trap door
26. Klaus, Violet, Sunny
27. Esmé
28. Cranberry juice
29. Room two
30. Stephano

31. Klaus and Violet
32. Green
33. None
34. Tin cans
35. Polly
36. Several hours
37. The library
38. Violet Baudelaire
39. Madame Lulu
40. A tattoo

41. A poncho
42. Chicken enchiladas
43. One
44. Duncan Quagmire, Isadora Quagmire
45. Start a fire
46. *Werewolves in the Rain*
47. Wine bottles
48. Duncan and Isadora
49. Toasted bread
50. Stockings

QUIZ 19

1. Wheat flour and batteries
2. Hal
3. Count Olaf
4. Elliot
5. The doorman
6. Montgomery
7. Esmé Squalor
8. Veblen Hall
9. Paperwork
10. White

11. Violet
12. A candelabra
13. The Incredibly Deadly Viper
14. In a theatre seat
15. Chilled cucumber soup
16. The curtains
17. Carmelita Spats
18. A pit
19. They have their hands tied behind their back during their meals
20. Violet's hair ribbon

21. Cold Lime Stew
22. Bricks and mortar
23. Sunny Baudelaire
24. The Volunteers Fighting Diseases

25. Captain Sham (Count Olaf)
26. Loud noises
27. Into a cave
28. Sunglasses
29. Captain Sham
30. A sword

31. Klaus
32. Sunny
33. Doctor Orwell
34. Cabbage sandwiches
35. Surgical masks
36. A hangman's noose
37. The red button
38. A shack
39. Lumpy oatmeal
40. Charles

41. The Incredibly Deadly Viper
42. A murder
43. The Cheer-up Cheeseburger
44. Hansel and Gretel
45. Foreman Firstein
46. The man with hooks for hands
47. A postman
48. Count Olaf
49. The Statue of Liberty
50. By welding

TRAGICALLY
TOUGH ANSWERS

QUIZ 1

1. The Fountain of Victorious Finance
2. Mrs Anwhistle
3. Secret Organizations You Should Know About
4. Inordinate
5. A burning torch
6. Rutabaga
7. Bruce
8. Young Rölf
9. An intercom
10. Albert, Edgar

11. Two pots
12. Scrambled eggs
13. The Valorous Farms Dairy
14. Ate it
15. Hotel Denouement
16. Ike
17. Rocks
18. Vertical Flame Diversion
19. Magenta wallpaper, billboards with weasels on them
20. The world is quiet here

21. Cynthia Vane
22. Warts
23. Six
24. She bit the snake on its nose

25. *The History of Lucky Smells Lumbermill*
26. A photograph of a new baby
27. Mount Fraught
28. Ophelia
29. Tony
30. Cake

31. Look! It Fits!
32. Can choose where they have dinner
33. C. M. Kornbluth
34. First Prize for Wretchedness
35. Geraldine Julienne
36. A bullfighter
37. The twelfth floor
38. The microphone
39. On the platform
40. The Virginian Wolfsnake

41. A notebook and pen
42. Paltryville
43. 1000
44. 10 minutes
45. Olivia
46. Nurse Flo
47. The Vineyard of Fragrant Grapes
48. A plank
49. Veblen Hall
50. The library